W9-BEV-652

Macmillan / McGraw-Hill

Linda Meeks
The Ohio State University

Philip Heit
The Ohio State University

**Macmillan
McGraw-Hill**

About the Authors

Professor Linda Meeks and Dr. Philip Heit

Linda Meeks and Philip Heit are emeritus professors of Health Education in the College of Education at The Ohio State University. As faculty members, Linda and Philip held joint appointments in Health Education in the College of Education and in Allied Medicine in the College of Medicine. Linda and Philip are America's most widely published health education co-authors. They have collaborated for more than 25 years, co-authoring more than 300 health books that are used by millions of students preschool through college. They are co-authors of an organized, sequential K–12 health education program, *Health and Wellness,* available from Macmillan/McGraw-Hill.

Together, they have helped state departments of education as well as thousands of school districts develop comprehensive school health education curricula. Their books and curricula are used throughout the United States, as well as in Canada, Japan, Mexico, England, Puerto Rico, Spain, Egypt, Jordan, Saudi Arabia, Bermuda, and the Virgin Islands. Linda and Philip train professors as well as educators in state departments of education and school districts. Their book, *Comprehensive School Health Education: Totally Awesome® Strategies for Teaching Health,* is the most widely used book for teacher training in colleges, universities, state departments of education, and school districts. Thousands of teachers around the world have participated in their *Totally Awesome® Teacher Training Workshops.* Linda and Philip have been the keynote speakers for many teacher institutes and wellness conferences. They are personally and professionally committed to the health and well-being of youth.

Chapter 6 outlines emergency care procedures that reflect the standard of knowledge and accepted practices in the United States at the time this book was published. It is the teacher's responsibility to stay informed of changes in emergency care procedures in order to teach current accepted practices. The teacher also can recommend that students gain complete, comprehensive training from courses offered by the American Red Cross.

The McGraw·Hill Companies

Macmillan McGraw-Hill

RFB&D
learning through listening

Published by Macmillan/McGraw-Hill, of McGraw-Hill Education, a division of The McGraw-Hill Companies, Inc., Two Penn Plaza, New York, New York 10121.

Students with print disabilities may be eligible to obtain an accessible, audio version of the pupil edition of this textbook. Please call Recording for the Blind & Dyslexic at 1-800-221-4792 for complete information.

Foldables™ and *Guidelines for Making Responsible Decisions*™ are trademarks of The McGraw-Hill Companies, Inc.

Printed in the United States of America   ISBN 0-02-284964-5/3

7 8 9 DOR 14 13 12 11 10

Contributors

Celan Alo, M.D., MPH
Medical Epidemiologist
Bureau of Chronic Disease and Tobacco
   Prevention
Texas Department of Health
Austin, Texas

Danny Ballard, Ed.D.
Associate Professor, Health
Texas A&M University
College of Education
College Station, Texas

Lucille Villegas Barrera, M.E.D.
Elementary Science Specialist
Houston Independent School District
Houston, Texas

Gus T. Dalis, Ed.D.
Consultant of Health Education
Torrance, California

Alisa Evans-Debnam, MPH
Dean of Health Programs
Fayetteville Technical Community College
Fayetteville, North Carolina

**Susan C. Giarratano-Russell,
MSPH, Ed.D., CHES**
Health Education, Evaluation & Media
   Consultant
National Center for Chronic Disease
   Prevention & Health Promotion
Centers for Disease Control & Prevention
Glendale, California

Donna Lloyd-Kolkin, Ph.D.
Principal Associate
Public Health Applications & Research
Abt Associates, Inc.
Bethesda, Maryland

Mulugheta Teferi, M.A.
Principal
Gateway Middle School
Center for Math, Science & Technology
St. Louis, Missouri

Roberto P. Treviño, M.D.
Director, Social & Health Research Center
Bienestar School-Based Diabetes
   Prevention Program
San Antonio, Texas

Dinah Zike, M.Ed.
Dinah Might Adventures LP
San Antonio, Texas

Content Reviewers

Mark Anderson
Supervisor, Health Physical
   Education
Cobb County Public
   Schools
Marietta, Georgia

Ken Ascoli
Assistant Principal
Our Lady of Fatima High
   School
Warren, Rhode Island

Jane Beougher, Ph.D.
Professor Emeritus of
   Health Education,
   Physical Education,
   and Education
Capital University
Westerville, Ohio

Lillie Burns
HIV/AIDS Prevention
   Education
Education Program
   Coordinator
Louisiana Department of
   Education
Baton Rouge, Louisiana

Jill English, Ph.D., CHES
Professor, Soka University
Aliso Viejo, California

Elizabeth Gallun, M.A.
Specialist, Comprehensive
   Health Education
Maryland State Department
   of Education
Baltimore, Maryland

Brenda Garza
Health Communications
   Specialist
Centers for Disease Control
   and Prevention
Atlanta, Georgia

Sheryl Gotts, M.S.
Consultant, Retired from
   Milwaukee Schools
Milwaukee, Wisconsin

Russell Henke, M.Ed.
Coordinator of Health
Montgomery County Public
   Schools
Rockville, Maryland

Kathy Kent
Health and Physical
   Education Teacher
Simpsonville Elementary
   School at Morton Place
Simpsonville, South
   Carolina

Bill Moser, M.S.
Program Specialist for
   Health and Character
   Education
Winston-Salem Forsyth City
   Schools
Winston-Salem, North
   Carolina

Debra Ogden
Curriculum Coordinator
District School Board of
   Collier County
Naples, Florida

Thurman Robins
Chair/Professor
Health and Kinesiology
   Department
Texas Southern University
Houston, Texas

**Sherman Sowby, Ph.D.,
CHES**
Professor, Department of
   Health Science
California State University,
   Fresno
Fresno, California

Greg Stockton
Health and Safety Expert
American Red Cross
Washington, D.C.

**Deitra Wengert, Ph.D.,
CHES**
Professor, Department of
   Health Science
Towson University
Towson, Maryland

**Susan Wooley-Goekler,
Ph.D., CHES**
Adjunct Faculty
Kent State University
Kent, Ohio

Medical Reviewers

Celan Alo, M.D., MPH
Medical Epidemiologist
Bureau of Chronic Disease
   and Tobacco Prevention
Texas Department of
   Health
Austin, Texas

**Donna Bacchi, M.D.,
MPH**
Associate Professor of
   Pediatrics
Director, Division of
   Community Pediatrics
Texas Tech University
Health Science Center
Lubbock, Texas

**Olga Dominguez
Satterwhite, R.D., L.D.**
Registered Dietitian and
   Diabetes Educator
Baylor College of Medicine
Houston, Texas

**Roberto P. Treviño,
M.D.**
Director, Social & Health
   Research Center
Bienestar School-Based
   Diabetes Prevention
   Program
San Antonio, Texas

iii

Contents

CHAPTER 2 Family and Social Health

 LOG ON www.mmhhealth.com
For more on Unit A Mental, Emotional, Family, and Social Health.

UNIT B Growth and Nutrition

CHAPTER 3 Growth and Development

CHAPTER 4 Nutrition

LOG ON www.mmhhealth.com
For more on Unit B Growth and Nutrition.

Personal Health and Safety

CHAPTER 5 Personal Health and Physical Activity

CHAPTER 6 Violence and Injury Prevention

LOG ON www.mmhhealth.com
For more on Unit C Personal Health and Safety.

Drugs and Disease Prevention

CHAPTER 7 Alcohol, Tobacco, and Other Drugs

LOG ON www.mmhhealth.com
For more on Unit D Drugs and Disease Prevention.

CHAPTER 9 Consumer and Community Health

LOG ON www.mmhhealth.com
For more on Unit E Community and
Environmental Health.

Features and Activities

UNIT C   Personal Health and Safety

Learning Life Skills
Use Communication Skills, **C36**
Set Health Goals, **C58**

Life Skills Activities
Make Responsible Decisions, **C8, C53**
Access Health Facts, Products, and Services,
   C13, C57
Be a Health Advocate, **C19, C77**
Manage Stress, **C23, C71**
Practice Healthful Behaviors, **C29, C47**
Resolve Conflicts, **C35**
Use Resistance Skills, **C63**
Analyze What Influences Your Health, **C67**

Build Character
Building a Safe Playground, **C31**
A Real Family, **C65**

Cross Curricular Links
Math, **C18**
Art, **C43**
Social Studies, **C45**
Physical Education, **C55**
Write About It!, **C12, C15, C61, C66**

On Your Own for School or Home
Choosing Physical Activities, **C28**
Surfer Safety Reminders, **C46**
Make a Poster, **C51**
Emergency Telephone Numbers, **C73**

Consumer Wise
Games That Improve Fitness Skills, **C25**

Health Online
Men, Women, and Body Fat, **C26**
Amber Alert System, **C62**

UNIT D   Drugs and Disease Prevention

Learning Life Skills
Use Resistance Skills, **D22**
Practice Healthful Behaviors, **D44**

Life Skills Activities
Be a Health Advocate, **D9**
Use Communication Skills, **D15**
Access Health Facts, Products, and Services, **D21**
Make Responsible Decisions, **D29, D53**
Resolve Conflicts, **D39**
Manage Stress, **D43**

Build Character
Pledge to Be Drug-Free, **D28**

Cross Curricular Links
Physical Education, **D12**
Science, **D13, D35, D42**
Art, **D19**

On Your Own for School or Home
Stop Germs! Poster, **D36**

Consumer Wise
Comparing Prices, **D5**
Investigate Food Labels, **D48**

Health Online
Caffeine: Then and Now, **D25**
Types of Diabetes, **D50**

Features and Activities

Life Skills

Life Skills are actions you can take to improve and maintain your health. The life skills that are taught in this text are listed below.

Using 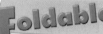 To help you learn these life skills, each of the Learning Life Skills features in this book include Foldables™. Foldables™ are three-dimensional graphic organizers you will make. They will help you understand the main points of each life skill.

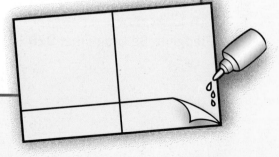

xvi

UNIT A

Mental, Emotional, Family, and Social Health

CHAPTER 1

Mental and Emotional Health

What Do You Know?

What do you know about mental and emotional health? Read the statements. Answer each one **yes** or **no**.

__?__ Talking about your feelings is healthful.

__?__ Your personality includes how you look, think, act, and feel.

__?__ Riding your bicycle without a helmet is a risk behavior.

__?__ People with good character don't mind if they break rules.

The answer to the first three statements is **yes**. The answer to the fourth statement is **no**. How did you do? You will learn more as you read this chapter, **Mental and Emotional Health**.

 LOG ON www.mmhhealth.com
Find out more about mental and emotional health.

Health Is Well-Being

You will learn . . .

- about the three parts of health.
- how choosing healthful behaviors protects your health.
- how choosing risk behaviors can harm your health.
- ten life skills that can help you take responsibility for your health.

Vocabulary

- **health**, *A5*
- **life skill**, *A7*
- **health goal**, *A8*
- **health behavior contract**, *A8*

What is well-being? It is having a healthy body. It is having a healthy mind. It is getting along with others.

The Three Parts of Health

Health is more than being free from illness. Health has three parts. **Health** is the condition of your body, mind, and relationships. All three parts of health affect your well-being.

The way you act, or *behave*, affects the three parts of health. You can learn how to make wise health choices. You can even set goals for better health. Behaving in healthful ways helps your health. This shows that you are responsible for your health.

 What are the three parts of health?

▼ Your well-being depends on the three parts of health working together.

Mental and emotional health is how well your mind works. It is how well you express your emotions. It is also how you feel about yourself.

Family and social health is how well you get along with others. It involves your relationships with family members, friends, and people in the community.

Physical health is how well your body works. A healthy body helps you do the things you want to do.

Healthful Behavior

Healthful behaviors are actions that can improve or protect your health. *Risk behaviors* are actions that can harm your health. When you brush your teeth, you practice a healthful behavior. You also take responsibility for your health. The chart below gives examples of both healthful and risk behaviors.

◀ **Wearing a bicycle helmet is a healthful behavior. In what other ways can you take responsibility for your health?**

Compare

Part of Health	Healthful Behavior	Risk Behavior
Physical Health	• Get enough sleep • Eat healthful foods • Play outdoors	• Stay up late • Eat foods high in fat and sugar • Watch too much television
Mental and Emotional Health	• Talk about your feelings • Do activities you enjoy • Learn about new things	• Ignore your feelings • Be bored • Refuse to try new things
Family and Social Health	• Help family members • Be kind to your friends • Avoid arguments with others	• Complain when a family member asks for help • Talk about your friends behind their backs • Fight with others

Life Skills for Health

A **life skill** is a healthful action you learn and practice for life. Each life skill gives you a way to take responsibility for your health. This book can help you learn how to use the ten life skills listed below.

- Access Health Facts, Products, and Services
- Practice Healthful Behaviors
- Manage Stress
- Analyze What Influences Your Health
- Use Communication Skills
- Use Resistance Skills
- Resolve Conflicts
- Set Health Goals
- Make Responsible Decisions
- Be a Health Advocate

 What is a life skill?

 **Write About It!**

Take Responsibility
Write a paragraph describing one way to take responsibility for health. Explain how this action can help you improve your physical, mental and emotional, and family and social health. Share your paragraph with a classmate.

Mental and Emotional Health

Family and Social Health

Physical Health

Set Health Goals

▼ A health behavior contract can help you set and meet goals. In step 3, tell who might help you reach your goal—a parent or guardian, a teacher, a family doctor, a school nurse, or a coach.

Setting health goals is an important part of health. A **health goal** is something you work toward in trying to stay healthy. You can use a health behavior contract to make a plan to reach a health goal. A **health behavior contract** is a written plan to help you practice a healthful behavior. Making a health behavior contract means taking responsibility for your health.

What is a health goal?

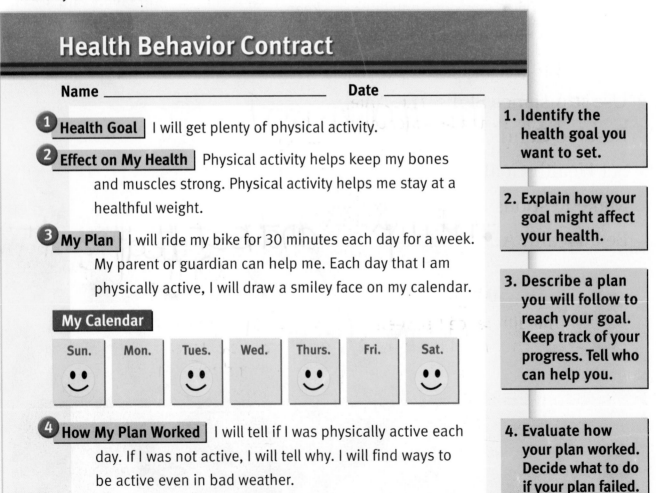

Health Behavior Contract

Name _____ Date _____

1 **Health Goal** | I will get plenty of physical activity.

2 **Effect on My Health** | Physical activity helps keep my bones and muscles strong. Physical activity helps me stay at a healthful weight.

3 **My Plan** | I will ride my bike for 30 minutes each day for a week. My parent or guardian can help me. Each day that I am physically active, I will draw a smiley face on my calendar.

My Calendar

Sun.	Mon.	Tues.	Wed.	Thurs.	Fri.	Sat.
:)		:)		:)		:)

4 **How My Plan Worked** | I will tell if I was physically active each day. If I was not active, I will tell why. I will find ways to be active even in bad weather.

1. Identify the health goal you want to set.

2. Explain how your goal might affect your health.

3. Describe a plan you will follow to reach your goal. Keep track of your progress. Tell who can help you.

4. Evaluate how your plan worked. Decide what to do if your plan failed.

A8

Set Health Goals

You want to improve your physical health. Begin by making a health behavior contract like the one on page A8. Then follow the steps for setting health goals.

1 **Write the health goal you want to set.**
I will get plenty of physical activity.

2 **Explain how your goal might affect your health.** In what ways can getting plenty of physical activity make you healthier?

3 **Describe a plan you will follow to reach your goal. Keep track of your progress.** Choose a physical activity you like. Plan to do it every day. Decide how you will keep track of your progress. Will you make a chart? Will you keep a log? Talk about your plan with a parent or guardian. Ask him or her to help you practice your health goal. Follow your plan for one week.

4 **Evaluate how your plan worked.** Are you following your health behavior contract? If not, what can you do to make your plan work?

LESSON REVIEW

Review Concepts

1. **Explain** the difference between mental and emotional health and family and social health.

2. **Explain** why riding a bicycle without a helmet is a risk behavior.

3. **Name** three healthful behaviors that you should do each day.

Critical Thinking

4. **Apply** Name three ways that you can take responsibility for your three parts of health.

5. **LIFE SKILLS** **Set Health Goals** Suppose you set a health goal to eat healthful snacks. What are four steps you can follow to reach this health goal?

A9

Your Self-Concept

You will learn . . .

- what makes you special.
- actions that help you have a healthful self-concept.
- about different ways that people learn.

Vocabulary

- **personality**, *A11*
- **heredity**, *A11*
- **self-concept**, *A12*
- **respect**, *A12*
- **rule**, *A12*

Think about the people you know. You are like some of those people in certain ways. In many ways, though, you are different. That's because there is only one you. You are one of a kind!

You Are Special

About 5 billion people live on planet Earth. Each one is special, including you! There never was and never will be another you. Your heredity, personality, talents, and skills make you special. No one else has exactly the same combination of these things as you.

 What is heredity?

Your talents and skills make you special. You may have musical or artistic talent. You may have skill in math or in certain sports.

Your personality makes you special. Your **personality** includes how you look, think, act, and feel. You may be shy or outgoing. You may like some parts of your personality. Other parts you may want to change.

Your heredity makes you special. Your **heredity** (huh•RED•ih•tee) is the traits you get from your birth parents. The color of your eyes and your height are two of these traits.

ACTIVITY

Art LINK

Self-Portrait

Draw a picture of yourself doing something you enjoy. Write a sentence telling why you enjoy this activity.

A Healthful Self-Concept

ACTIVITY

Music
L I N K

Respectful Rap

Write a rap song that describes how to show respect for others. Perform your rap for the class.

Your **self-concept** is the feelings you have about yourself. When you have a healthful self-concept, you have respect for yourself. Here are some actions that show you have a healthful self-concept.

- **Show respect for yourself and others.** **Respect** is treating others as you want to be treated. *Self-respect* is thinking highly of yourself. When you respect others, you treat them fairly. Following rules is one way to show respect for others. A **rule** is a guide to help you do the right thing.

When you have self-respect, you recognize your strengths. You learn from your mistakes. You work on your weaknesses.

▶ Taking care of your belongings shows self-respect.

A12

- **Practice life skills for health.** This shows that you care about your health. Respecting your health is part of respecting yourself.

- **Do your best.** You do some things very well. These are your strengths. You are not as good at other things. These are your weaknesses. Doing your best means working to improve both your strengths and weaknesses. This helps you to have a healthful self-concept.

Healthful Choices

Your actions show that you have self-respect and a healthful self-concept. You make responsible choices about how you live your life. You choose healthful behaviors over risk behaviors. You care about your health.

 How does practicing life skills show self-respect?

Health Online

Feeling Good About You

People with a healthful self-concept make healthful choices. Research the relationship between self-concept and choice. Use the e-Journal writing tool to write a report on your findings. Visit **www.mmhhealth.com** and click on ⓔ-Journal.

▼ **Grooming is an action that shows self-respect.**

Practice Healthful Behavior

Setting goals and practicing healthful behaviors can help you do your best. To practice healthful behaviors, follow the steps listed on the clipboard.

Learning Styles

Do you do your best to study and learn? Did you know that people study and learn in different ways? Some people learn best by listening. Some people learn best by doing what's required. Others learn best by writing things down. There are several different ways to learn. These are called *learning styles*. If you find your learning style, you can improve your grades.

✓ **Name one way to do your best.**

◀ Ask questions when you are unsure of something in class. This shows that you care about your schoolwork and want to do your best.

Practice Healthful Behaviors

Practicing healthful behaviors can help you learn. Use this activity to get started.

1 **Learn about a healthful behavior.** Make a list of activities that can help you learn. You might list studying with a friend or reading aloud. Choose one activity that seems to work well for you.

2 **Practice the behavior.** Practice the activity for three days. Keep a record to make sure you do the behavior each day.

3 **Ask for help if you need it. A parent or guardian can help.**

4 **Make the behavior a habit.** Focus on the activity you choose. Then pick a different way to learn and try again.

LESSON REVIEW

Review Concepts

1. **Name** what makes a person special.

2. **Identify** actions you can take to have a healthful self-concept.

3. **Define** learning style.

Critical Thinking

4. **Synthesize** You have tried to learn multiplication by reading. What other methods could you use to learn it?

5. **Practice Healthful Behaviors** You want to learn the correct way to floss your teeth. Who could help you?

A15

Your Mind and Emotions

You will learn . . .

- how to share emotions in healthful ways.
- how to use I-messages.
- ways to stay in a good mood.
- ways to keep your mind healthy.

Vocabulary

- **emotion**, *A17*
- **self-control**, *A18*
- **I-message**, *A18*
- **attitude**, *A20*

Look at this picture. You can tell what the girl is doing. Can you tell what she is feeling? You can if you look closely at her face. The expression on her face shows how she feels.

Your Emotions

To maintain health, you need to show emotion in healthful ways. An **emotion** is a feeling inside you. There are many kinds of emotions. Here are some healthful ways to express emotions.

- **Fear** Talk to your parents or guardian. Be honest. The adult may be able to help you get over your fear.

- **Caring** Caring is showing concern for others. If you care for someone, tell him or her. He or she may feel the same way about you.

- **Sadness or Grief** *Grief* means a feeling of being very sad. People feel grief over a loss, such as when a pet dies. They may feel grief when they are disappointed. Let your emotions out by crying. Talk to a responsible adult about the pain you feel. Keep a private journal.

- **Joy and Happiness** When you feel joy and happiness, show it. Don't try to hide how you feel. Smile or laugh. Your joy and happiness could make others feel happy.

 What are emotions?

Angry Feelings

Sending I-messages

- **Tell what has happened.**
- **Tell how it affects you.**
- **Tell how you feel.**

Suppose a friend makes you angry. You need to share your angry feelings in healthful ways.

Self-control helps you share your angry feelings in a healthful way. **Self-control** is having control over your emotions and actions. Taking deep breaths and counting to ten may help you keep your self-control when you are angry. Another way to express angry feelings is by using an I-message. An **I-message** is a healthful way to talk about feelings when you are upset.

✔ **What is self-control?**

It hurt.

◀ **Suppose you are playing tennis. You get hit with the ball. You feel angry. You might use the I-message below.**

What Happened	How It Affected You	How You Felt
When the tennis ball hit me . . .	. . . it hurt . . .	. . . and I felt angry.

How You Feel

Your *mood* is the way you feel at a certain time. There are ways to stay in a good mood.

- **Get physical activity.** Your brain makes special chemicals when you exercise. These can lift your mood.

- **Do something well.** Being successful makes you feel good about yourself.

- **Spend time with people who care about you.** These people can help you stay in a good mood during hard times.

- **Help someone else.** This helps you both stay in a good mood.

 How can you stay in a good mood?

▶ Helping someone can help you both stay in a good mood.

CRITICAL THINKING

Use Communication Skills

Your brother used your baseball mitt without asking. You are angry. Use communication skills to share your emotions. Work with a partner to role-play these steps.

1. **Choose the best way to communicate.** How will you tell your brother you are angry? Will you yell and scream? Will you talk about how you are feeling?

2. **Send a clear message. Be polite.** Write an I-message to tell your brother how you feel. Be direct.

3. **Listen to each other.** Say your I-message. Then listen to your brother. Maybe he had a good reason for using your mitt.

4. **Make sure you understand each other.** Tell your brother what you heard. Ask what he heard from you. How can you improve your communication skills?

A Healthy Mind

A healthful attitude helps keep your mind healthy. Your **attitude** is the way you think, act, or feel.

If you have a healthful attitude, you think about things in a healthful way. Suppose your parents or guardian tell you that you have to do chores. You do the chores as a way to help your family. You carry them out cheerfully. You have a healthful attitude. These are ways to keep your mind healthy.

Avoid Worry

You may worry before you take a test. You may feel anxious when you perform a play for a group of people. Worrying too much can harm your mental and emotional health. Worry also can harm your physical health. It can cause your body to feel tense and tired. It may cause you to become ill. You can talk to your parents or guardian when you are worried. They can help you relax. They can help you let go of your worry. Letting go will help your mental and emotional and physical health.

ACTIVITY

Consumer Wise

Media Messages

Sometimes ads cause people to worry. Work with a partner. Cut out ads from old newspapers and magazines. Which ads cause you to worry? Which don't? Paste the ads on poster board to show how they are different.

Keep Sharp

Learning new things helps keep your mind sharp. You can learn by reading books, talking with others, and building friendships. Get plenty of physical activity, rest, and sleep, too. Your mind is alert when you are well-rested. You can think clearly. You can perform better.

Avoid Drugs

Stay away from drugs and chemicals. Some drugs can have a harmful effect on the mind. They cause your thinking to be slow and cloudy. Chemicals such as cleaning products, paint, or glue can be harmful. These products should be used in a well-ventilated area. Opening a window can help.

 What is a healthful attitude?

Math LINK

ACTIVITY

Build Your Math Memory

Write multiplication facts and their products on separate cards. Place all the cards facedown. Turn over two cards. If they show a fact and its product, pick up the cards. If not, put them back facedown and try again.

LESSON REVIEW

Review Concepts

1. **Describe** one way you can share emotions in a healthful way.

2. **Define** an I-message.

3. **Name** two things you can do to stay in a healthful mood.

4. **Name** three things you can do to keep your mind healthy.

Critical Thinking

5. **Apply** Suppose your best friend is moving away. You are sad. What are some ways you can stay in a healthful mood?

6. **LIFE SKILLS** **Use Communication Skills** Suppose a friend borrowed a special pen from you and then lost it. Write an I-message that tells your friend how you feel.

Good Character Matters

Have you ever wished that you could be a superhero? You can! By showing good character, you can be your own superhero every day.

citizenship

caring

responsibility

trustworthiness

respect

fairness

Good Character

Do you tell the truth? Are you kind to others? Your actions can show that you have good character. **Good character** is acting in ways that show healthful traits, such as caring and respect. Other healthful traits are trustworthiness, responsibility, citizenship, and fairness.

If you have good character, you are trustworthy. You always tell the truth. You respect other people by treating them the way you want to be treated. You are responsible. You can be counted on to do what you say you will do. You do your part to make the world a better place. You are fair and share things evenly. You are caring and kind to others.

Good character is something you can show every day. Sometimes it is easy to show good character. Sometimes it is not easy. Showing good character takes self-control.

 List the six traits of good character.

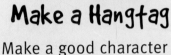 **Art LINK**

Make a Hangtag

Make a good character hangtag. A hangtag is a sign that can be hung on a doorknob. Cut a hangtag out of cardboard. Use a marker to write "Hang on to Good Character" at the top. Then write:

- I will tell the truth.
- I will show respect.
- I will be fair.

Hang your tag where you can see it to remind you of good character.

Hang on to good character.
☆ I will tell the truth.
☆ I will show respect.
☆ I will be fair.

◀ **Do your actions at school show that you have good character?**

Write About It!

What I Admire About You Write a letter to your friend. In your letter tell your friend what parts of his or her character you admire. Tell your friend how he or she has been your hero.

Friends with Good Character

Think about one of your friends. Try to remember when you first met. Did you try to learn about this person? Did you listen to what the person said? Did you watch the person's actions?

Your friend's words and actions showed his or her values. **Values** are ideas that guide the way a person acts. Some people think being kind is important. Others believe it is important to work hard.

These are examples of values. You probably make friends with people who have the same values as you. You agree on what is important. You agree on how to live your life.

A **hero** is a person you look up to because of what he or she stands for or has done. A hero should show healthful values and good character.

Who are your heroes? Do your heroes' actions show his or her values?

◄ **How do your friends show good character?**

Choosing Friends

It is important to choose friends with good character. Friends with good character will suggest healthful activities for you to do together. They will not tempt you into wrong actions. How do you know if a friend has good character? Choose friends who

- practice healthful behaviors and avoid risk behaviors.

- make responsible decisions.

- say "no" when asked to do something wrong.

- tell when they have done something wrong and try to make up for it.

- do not resolve conflict by fighting.

It is not always easy to hang on to good character. Friends, though, can help each other. You and your friends can be health advocates. You can follow the steps in the activity at right.

 What are two traits to look for in a friend?

ACTIVITY
LIFE SKILLS
CRITICAL THINKING

Be a Health Advocate

You can be an advocate for good character. Work with a partner and follow the steps below.

1 **Choose a healthful action to communicate.** Which trait of good character do you think is most important in school? Choose one of the traits to practice and support.

2 **Collect information about the action.** Think about ways you and your classmates can practice the trait you chose. Write them down.

3 **Decide how to communicate this information.** Write a script or a public service announcement.

4 **Communicate your message to others.** Follow through on your plan. Perform your ideas for your classmates.

Showing Respect

Social Studies LINK

Explore a World of Ways to Show Respect

People of other cultures may have different ways of showing respect. One way Japanese people show respect is to bow. Choose a culture you want to learn about. Find out how the people show respect. Act out your findings for the class.

If you have good character, your actions show respect. You can show respect for your family members by following their rules. You can show respect for your friends by helping them. You can show respect for your classmates and teachers by using manners. Others remember these actions. They know that you think highly of them. Their respect for you will grow in return.

What If I Do Something Wrong?

Everyone makes mistakes. Sometimes a mistake happens because you made an unwise choice. Sometimes a mistake happens by accident. Either way, you need to correct the mistake. You need to take action.

▶ You can show respect by talking politely to another person.

Suppose your friend just got a new game. You borrow it and lose one of the pieces. You need to correct the mistake. First you **apologize**, or say you are sorry. Tell your friend you are sorry, and mean it. Then you take action to make it up to him. Maybe you buy a new game for your friend. Maybe you give your friend one of your games. Maybe you ask an adult to help you make a piece like the one you lost.

You have corrected your mistake. It is important to try to avoid making the same mistake again. You could try not to borrow others' things. When you have to borrow something, you take care of it.

✓ **What should you do if you do something wrong?**

▲ Suppose someone broke a friend's wagon. What should he or she do?

LESSON REVIEW

Review Concepts

1. **Identify** the six traits of good character.

2. **Tell** why you might want to choose friends who share your values.

3. **Explain** how apologizing to someone when you make a mistake shows good character.

Critical Thinking

4. **Evaluate** Choose one of the six traits of good character. Why is this an important trait for a friend to have? Explain your answer.

5. **LIFE SKILLS** **Be a Health Advocate** You want to practice citizenship at school. Explain how you and your classmates could advocate for making school a safer place.

Making Responsible Decisions

You will learn . . .

- what questions to ask before you make a decision.
- ways to communicate with responsible adults about health decisions.
- how to use resistance skills.

Vocabulary

- **responsible decision**, *A29*
- **resistance skills**, *A30*

You make decisions every day. Even simple decisions, like how to spend your free time, affect your health. In this lesson you can learn how to make decisions that help you stay healthy.

Responsible Decisions

A **responsible decision** is a choice you make that is safe and healthful and follows family guidelines. Making responsible decisions can help you stay healthy. You also make your parents or guardian proud.

Sometimes it is hard to make a responsible decision. Answering the six questions listed on the clipboard will help. A "no" answer to one or more of the questions shows that a decision is not responsible.

In making a hard decision, ask your parents or guardian or another responsible adult for help. Tell the adult all the facts. Tell him or her the choices that you might make. Ask the adult what he or she would do. Listen carefully, and make sure you understand the answer. Then make a responsible decision.

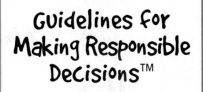

Guidelines for Making Responsible Decisions™

1. Is it healthful?
2. Is it safe?
3. Does it follow rules and laws?
4. Does it show respect for myself and others?
5. Does it follow my family's guidelines?
6. Does it show good character?

 Tell why wearing safety gear when skating is a responsible decision.

Resistance Skills

Write About It!

How to Say "No" Write a "How To" paragraph listing the steps used to say "no." Include what you should do at each step. Share your writing with the class.

Suppose your friend asks you to go swimming. There will not be any adults watching. You review the *Guidelines for Making Responsible Decisions*™. You answer "no" to at least one question. You decide not to go swimming with your friend. How can you tell him your decision? You can use resistance skills. **Resistance skills** are ways to say "no" to unwise decisions.

Resisting Risk Behaviors

When you use resistance skills, you say "no" in a firm voice. You also give reasons for your decision. One reason might be that swimming with no adults watching breaks a rule. Healthful behaviors follow rules. Risk behaviors go against rules.

▶ **Make sure your actions match your words when you say "no."**

Next you act on your words. You know it is unsafe to swim alone, so you decide to ride your bike instead. You do not let your friend talk you into swimming. It also is important to tell an adult about his unwise decision.

 What are resistance skills?

LIFE SKILLS

CRITICAL THINKING

Use Resistance Skills

Work with a partner to practice using resistance skills. Suppose a classmate wants to copy your answers during a test. First, write about how you would say "no." Include reasons you would give for your decision. Then, role-play the situation with your partner. Follow the steps for using resistance skills.

1. **Look at the person. Say "no" in a firm voice.**

2. **Give reasons for saying "no."**

3. **Match your behavior to your words.**

4. **Ask an adult for help if you need it.**

LESSON REVIEW

Review Concepts

1. **List** six questions to ask when you have to make a hard decision.

2. **Explain** how to ask for help when making a responsible decision.

3. **Describe** when you should use resistance skills.

4. **List** the steps to use to say "no."

Critical Thinking

5. **Predict** Your friend wants you to walk to his house but it's dark. Use the *Guidelines for Making Responsible Decisions*™. What might happen if you choose to go? What might happen if you use resistance skills instead?

6. **LIFE SKILLS** **Use Resistance Skills** Suppose that when telling a friend "no," you begin to laugh. Do you think your friend will believe your words? Tell why or why not.

Make Responsible Decisions

Problem María's friend wants her to take a shortcut through an unsafe place. What should she do?

> I'm not sure that's a good idea. I do want more time to ride our bikes, though.

> I know a shortcut home. We can go through the lot where they tore down the factory. We'll get home faster and have more time to ride our bikes!

Guidelines for Making Responsible Decisions™

- Is it healthful?
- Is it safe?
- Does it follow rules and laws?
- Does it show respect for me and others?
- Does it follow family guidelines?
- Does it show good character?

Solution María has the responsibility of staying safe. She decides to use the four steps on the next page to make a responsible decision.

Learn This Life Skill

Follow these steps to make responsible decisions. The Foldables™ can help.

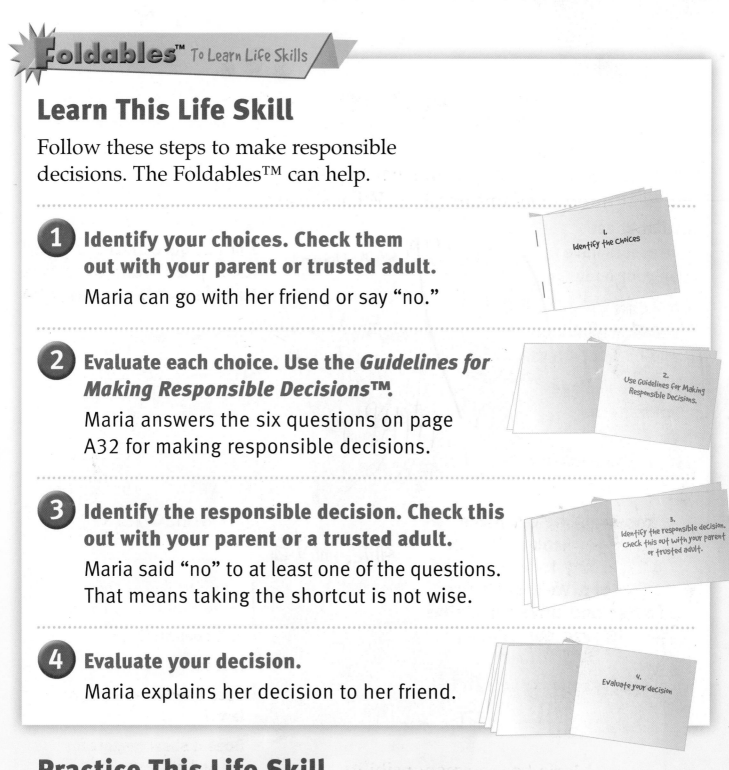

1 **Identify your choices. Check them out with your parent or trusted adult.**

Maria can go with her friend or say "no."

2 **Evaluate each choice. Use the *Guidelines for Making Responsible Decisions™*.**

Maria answers the six questions on page A32 for making responsible decisions.

3 **Identify the responsible decision. Check this out with your parent or a trusted adult.**

Maria said "no" to at least one of the questions. That means taking the shortcut is not wise.

4 **Evaluate your decision.**

Maria explains her decision to her friend.

Practice This Life Skill

Write down a time when you made a hard decision. Swap with a classmate. Make a responsible decision using the steps above.

Manage Stress

You will learn . . .

- what effect stressors have on your body.
- the difference between healthful and harmful stress.
- ways to manage your stress.

Vocabulary

- **stress**, *A35*
- **stressor**, *A35*
- **healthful stress**, *A36*
- **harmful stress**, *A37*

The people in your life expect a lot from you. You also expect a lot from yourself. You want to be the best person you can be. Sometimes it is hard to do everything well. Sometimes trying too hard affects your health.

Stressors

Stress is the way your body reacts when there are changes in your life. Everyone feels stress. It is a natural part of life. That's because you deal with stressors every day. A **stressor** is something that causes stress. Every person has different stressors. Talking in front of the class might be a stressor for you. It might not bother someone else. The sound of a baby crying might not cause you stress. This sound, though, probably is a stressor to the baby's parents or guardian.

Stress causes changes in your body. These changes can help you get ready for quick action. Look at the photo of the student. He feels stress. Read about what is happening to his body because of stress.

Good changes can cause stress. They cause your body to react. Getting an "A" on a test, adopting a new kitten, or buying a new skateboard might be stressors.

 What is a stressor?

Effects of Stress

- **Your heart may beat faster to pump blood to your muscles.**
- **You may breathe faster to get more oxygen.**
- **Sugar stored in your body enters the blood to give you more energy.**
- **Your hands get sweaty.**
- **Your knees feel shaky.**

The Two Types of Stress

Stress can be healthful. **Healthful stress** is stress that helps you perform well. It also helps keep you healthy.

Suppose you are a pitcher on a baseball team. Your team will win the game if you strike out the next batter. You feel stress. You breathe faster to get more oxygen. Your heart beats faster. Your body releases sugar into your blood. This sugar gives you energy. You throw the ball faster than ever before. The batter strikes out, and your team wins the game.

Your body changed due to stress. These changes gave you energy and helped you perform better. The stress was healthful.

▼ **What may be a stressor to one person might not be a stressor to another person. Why might that be?**

Harmful Stress

Sometimes stress is harmful. **Harmful stress** is stress that harms health or causes you to perform poorly.

Suppose you are in a school play. You have not practiced your lines. You are worried about how you will do. You have trouble falling asleep. On the day of the performance you get a stomachache. Just before the play starts, your head starts to hurt. You cannot remember your lines.

Harmful stress caused changes in your body. You had trouble sleeping. You got a stomachache and a headache. If the stress continues, it could lead to illness.

 What are some ways that harmful stress affects the mind and body?

 CAREERS

School Counselor

School counselors help students when they are in school. They can help students with many kinds of problems. For example, they help students manage stress. They also help students plan for their future.

School counselors must have at least a four-year college degree. They may have even more training. They must be certified.

If you are interested in helping people, think about being a school counselor.

LOG ON www.mmhhealth.com Find out more about other careers in health.

◀ **Students who feel stress can get help from counselors at school. Many youth clubs and community centers have counselors who can help.**

A37

Managing Stress

Manage Stress

1. Identify the signs of stress.

2. Identify the cause of stress.

3. Do something about the cause of stress.

4. Take action to reduce the harmful effects of stress.

When you feel stress, talk to parents or guardians. Other trusted adults to talk to are

- teachers
- school counselors
- school nurse
- family doctor
- health clinic health professionals
- community center professionals
- youth club counselors

Whenever you experience stress, be aware of the signs. Then identify what you think is causing the stress. Try to do something about the cause. Failing to practice lines for the school play can cause stress. You can talk to your parents or guardian about stress. They can help you decide what to do about the cause of stress. You may not know what is causing stress. They can help you figure it out.

▲ Getting plenty of sleep is one way to manage stress.

Reducing Stress

You can take action to reduce the harmful effects of stress.

- Get plenty of rest and sleep.

- Get plenty of physical activity each day.

- Eat healthful meals and snacks.

- Take slow, deep breaths. This slows down your heart rate and blood pressure.

- Take time during the day to relax.

 Describe two actions to manage harmful stress.

LIFE SKILLS **ACTIVITY** **CRITICAL THINKING**

Manage Stress

Your book report for school is due tomorrow. You haven't finished reading the book yet. You have a stomachache and feel tired. Work with a partner. Act out ways to reduce stress for your class.

1. **Identify the signs of stress.** What signs show you are under stress? Act these signs out.

2. **Identify the cause of stress.** Talk to your partner about what's causing this stress.

3. **Do something about the cause of stress.** With your partner, make a plan that would help you get your report done.

4. **Take action to reduce the harmful effects of stress.** With your partner, determine how you can reduce stress and still get your report done. Act out your ideas for the class.

LESSON REVIEW

Review Concepts

1. **List** ways your body changes because of stress.

2. **Contrast** healthful stress and harmful stress.

3. **Explain** how getting rest, getting physical activity, and eating healthful foods can help you manage the effects of stress.

Critical Thinking

4. **Analyze** How might a school counselor help you manage stress?

5. **LIFE SKILLS** **Manage Stress** A friend is feeling the effects of harmful stress. What are some things she can do to reduce the effects of stress?

Use Vocabulary

attitude, *A20*

good character, *A23*

harmful stress, *A37*

health goal, *A8*

respect, *A12*

responsible
  decision, *A29*

Choose the correct term from the list to complete each sentence.

1. Treating others as you want to be treated is __?__.

2. The way you think, act, or feel is your __?__.

3. Something you work toward to help you become a healthier person is a(n) __?__.

4. Stress that can cause you to perform poorly is __?__.

5. A safe and healthful choice is a(n) __?__.

6. Acting in ways that show healthful traits, such as caring and respect, is __?__.

Review Concepts

Answer each question in complete sentences.

7. What is an example of a risk behavior?

8. What does the first part of an I-message describe?

9. What are three important things to do when you make a mistake?

10. How can healthful stress help you perform well?

Reading Comprehension

Answer each question in complete sentences.

Doing your best includes doing your best in school. People study and learn in different ways. Some people learn best by listening. Some people learn best by reading. Others learn best by writing things down. These different ways to learn are called learning styles.

11. What is a learning style?

12. What are three ways people learn?

13. How can discovering your learning style help you do your best?

Critical Thinking/Problem Solving

Answer each question in complete sentences.

Analyze Concepts

14. Why is it important to care for the three parts of health?

15. Explain how to make a health behavior contract.

16. How does using communication skills show good character?

17. How can you have a good attitude about studying?

18. How can you show family members that you are fair?

Practice Life Skills

19. **Use Communication Skills** A friend promised to help you study for a test. The day before the test, he called and said he was going to a movie instead. You are angry. Write an I-message to your friend about how you feel.

20. **Make Responsible Decisions** Think about a hard decision you have made or need to make. List the *Guidelines for Making Responsible Decisions*™ and your answer to each question. Describe the decision you made. Give reasons for your choice.

Read Graphics

Use the chart to answer questions 21–23.

Derek's Ways to Show Good Character	
Quality	**Action**
Trustworthiness	Always tell my parents the truth about where I am going.
Respect	Ask before I borrow from someone.
Responsibility	Turn in my homework on time.
Citizenship	Do something to help in my community.
Fairness	Let my friends play with my toys and games.
Caring	Do something to help children or older adults.

21. Name one other action Derek could include to show trustworthiness.

22. Derek wants to start a food drive project in his class. Which quality would this action be listed as?

23. Derek reads a book to his younger sister at night. Which qualities might this action relate to?

 LOG ON www.mmhhealth.com
Find out how much you know about mental and emotional health.

CHAPTER 2

Family and Social Health

You're Invited

Family

What Do You Know?

People who are in healthful relationships respect each other. Read each statement. Write **yes** if you agree. Write **no** if you disagree.

Respect means:

_?_ treating others as you would like to be treated.

_?_ helping your family with chores.

_?_ listening to your friends ideas.

Did you answer **yes** to each statement? Great! All these statements tell ways to show respect. To learn more about healthful relationships read **Family and Social Health**.

www.mmhhealth.com
Find out more about family and social health.

A43

Healthful Relationships

You will learn . . .

- ways to make a healthful relationship.
- ways to show respect for other people.
- how to communicate in healthful ways.

Vocabulary

- **relationship**, *A45*
- **respect**, *A45*
- **communicate**, *A47*
- **body language**, *A47*

Think about the people in your life. You have family members and friends. You have teachers and classmates. You have a relationship with all those people.

Relationships and Respect

A **relationship** is a connection you have with another person. You have many kinds of relationships. You have relationships with family members, friends, teachers, classmates, and neighbors.

In a healthful relationship, there is respect. **Respect** is treating others as you want to be treated. There also is communication.

Respecting Other People

You can show respect in these ways.

- **Show good character.** Do not ask others to do anything wrong. Do not ask friends to break school rules. Encourage your friends to show good character.

- **Follow family guidelines.** Show respect for your *family guidelines,* or rules set by parents or guardians that tell you how to act. Do not break rules. Don't do something you know you shouldn't do.

- **Help others stay healthy.** Encourage friends to eat healthful snacks instead of junk food, for example.

BUILD **ACTIVITY**

Character

Make a Chart

Respect Make a four-column chart. Write "Family," "Friends," "Teachers," and "Self" across the top of each column. List five actions that show respect for your family, friends, teachers, and yourself. Hang the chart where you can see it. Try to show respect everyday in these ways.

Write About It!

Communicate with Respect Write a paragraph about showing respect to your teacher when you communicate. Present your paragraph to the class. Show how you are respectful when you communicate to your teacher.

- **Choose actions that keep people safe.** Follow safety rules in the classroom and on the playground.
- **Avoid violence.** *Violence* is harm done to yourself, others, or property. Kicking, pushing, or punching is violence. Taking things from others is violence.

Getting Respect from Other People

In healthful relationships, other people respect you. Here are some ways to get respect.

- **Have self-respect.** *Self-respect* is thinking highly of yourself. When you show self respect, others will show respect for you.
- **Set limits.** To *set limits* is to say what actions are OK and not OK with you.
- **Use honest talk.** Tell others how you feel. Maybe someone did not show respect for you. You might feel angry or hurt.
- **Ask others to change disrespectful action.** If someone shoves you, tell him or her not to do it ever again.

When people respect each other they can work together better. When you do the activities in this book with your classmates, follow all the ways of giving and getting respect. You'll find you can do the activities faster and better.

▼ **Helping family members shows respect. In what other ways might you show respect at home?**

 What is a relationship?

Healthful Communication

Healthful relationships are built on good communication. When you **communicate**, you share feelings, thoughts, or information. There are two parts to communication: sending messages and listening.

Three Ways to Send Messages

Good communication is getting your message across.

- **Speaking and Writing** You might speak to someone or send an email. You could write a note, or draw a picture. When talking with someone, be polite. Use correct grammar. Give the person your full attention. Use I-messages to say how you feel.

- **Body Language** The way you move your body to communicate is called **body language**. The way you use your hands and arms sends a message to others. The look on your face and the way you sit and stand sends a message, too.

- **Sign Language** People who cannot hear use their hands to communicate. This is called *sign language*.

write About It!

Ways to Say "I'm Sorry" Think of a time when someone you know hurt a friend. Maybe the person teased his or her friend. The friend's feelings were hurt. Work with a partner. Write several ways to say "I'm sorry" such as "I apologize for being mean." Then take turns role-playing your ideas.

BUILD ACTIVITY

Character

Respect Our Teacher

Respect Do a role-play with a group. Show how to use respect when group members communicate with your teacher.

A47

Two Ways to Show You Are Listening

When you listen, you can show that you hear and understand.

- **Give the other person your full attention.** When the other person speaks, look directly at him or her. Let the person finish before you begin to talk. If you are talking on the telephone, don't watch television at the same time.

- **Pay attention to body language.** Remember, your body language sends messages. Are you smiling when you listen? Are you frowning? Are you tapping your foot? What messages do these actions send? Be aware of the other person's body language, too. Is the person interested or bored?

✔ **Tell some healthful ways to share what you feel, think, and know.**

► When listening to someone, give the person your full attention. Look at her.

Use Communication Skills

Using your own words to repeat what another person says helps communication. This is called *paraphrasing*. Work with a partner. Role-play this skill.

1 **Choose the best way to communicate.** Say or read a sentence to your partner. You might want to choose a sentence from a book.

2 **Send a clear message. Be polite.** Speak clearly. Look at your partner.

3 **Listen to each other.** Have your partner paraphrase what you said. How did your partner do?

4 **Make sure you understand each other.** Talk about how well you communicated. Did your partner understand you? How could you make what you said clearer? How could your partner listen better? Switch roles and try the activity again.

LESSON REVIEW

Review Concepts

1. **List** three ways you might show respect for others.

2. **Describe** three ways you might get respect from others.

3. **Define** the term body language.

Critical Thinking

4. **Analyze** You do not ask your friends to do something wrong. How does this show respect?

5. **LIFE SKILLS** **Use Communication Skills** You tell Nathan to meet you near the swings. Nathan looks for you near the slide. What might have caused the mix up?

Resolving Conflict

You will learn . . .

- how to apply the four steps to resolve conflict.
- ways to get along with others.
- how peer pressure works.

Vocabulary

- **conflict**, *A51*
- **peer**, *A54*
- **peer pressure**, *A54*

Sometimes people disagree. This can lead to conflict. You can learn to resolve conflicts without fighting.

How to Resolve Conflict

A disagreement is a **conflict**. Some conflicts are easy to handle. Other conflicts might be harder to handle. They might include angry feelings. There are four steps you can use to resolve conflict. Using the steps shows respect and keeps relationships healthful.

Steps to Resolve Conflict

1. **Stay calm.** Do not act on any strong feelings.

2. **Talk about the conflict.** Use I-messages to tell what you are feeling. Allow time for each person to speak.

3. **List possible ways to settle the conflict.** Work together to find ways to resolve the conflict. Check out each way to settle the conflict using the *Guidelines for Making Responsible Decisions*™.

4. **Agree on a way to settle the conflict. You may need to ask a responsible adult for help.** Agree on the best solution. If you need help, ask a responsible adult.

 Why are some conflicts harder to resolve than others?

Resolve Conflicts

1. **Stay calm.**

2. **Talk about the conflict.**

3. **List possible ways to settle the conflict.**

4. **Agree on a way to settle the conflict. You may need to ask a responsible adult for help.**

Getting Along with Others

Being fair means following rules, taking turns, and sharing. Being fair helps you get along better with others. When you are not fair, conflict can happen.

Ways to Get Along with Others

Here are some other actions you can take.

- **Think about your actions.** How will they affect other people? Put yourself in their shoes. How would you feel?

- **Show respect.** Do not use or borrow items without asking.

- **Share.** Take only your portion. Share what you have with others.

- **Take turns.** Taking turns is one of the easiest ways to be fair.

- **Play by the rules.** Follow family guidelines and school rules. Do not cheat when playing games or doing homework.

- **Do not *gossip*, or say unkind words, about others.** Gossip can hurt other people's feelings. It can also change the way people see you. They might think you can't be trusted.

▼ When playing on a team, always play fair. Follow the rules.

The Harmful Effects of Gossip

When you gossip you change the way people think about you. Some people may think that if you gossip about others, you gossip about them, too. Here is what can happen if you gossip.

- **People will not trust you if you gossip.** Suppose a friend tells you something that upset her. You tell other classmates. If your friend finds out, she will no longer trust you. You could even lose her as a friend.

- **People will have hurt feelings if you gossip.** Suppose a friend gets a new haircut. You make fun of his new haircut to another friend. He hears what you said. He now has hurt feelings.

- **People can get angry.** Suppose you tell others something that isn't true about a classmate. How do you think she might feel? She might feel hurt. She might get angry. She might try to get even with you.

- **People might think you are disrespectful or a coward.** Suppose a classmate does something that you do not like. You tell others, but you don't tell him. He finds out what you said. He might think you are a coward. You did not tell him how you felt.

 What is gossip?

Con$umer Wi$e

Go to the store with your parents or guardian. Look for games and activities in which players work together. You might see competitive games. *Competitive* means someone wins, and someone loses. You will also see activities, such as games and puzzles, where people work together. When people work together, they *cooperate*. Write down the cooperative games you find.

What to Do About Peer Pressure

A **peer** is someone who is the same age as you. Sometimes peers try to get you to act or think a certain way. The effect that other children your age have on you is called **peer pressure**.

There are two types of peer pressure: positive and negative. Positive peer pressure is healthful. For example, friends might influence you to do your homework on time.

Negative peer pressure can be harmful. Being pressured to cheat or lie are examples of negative peer pressure. Avoid peers who try to use negative peer pressure against you.

When Someone Wants to Fight

A *fight* is a struggle between two or more people. A fight might be with words. It might include yelling. A fight might involve punching, shoving, and kicking. A peer who threatens or frightens others is a *bully*. People who are bullied often feel alone, very sad, and confused.

If someone wants to fight, say that you do not want to fight. Get away from the situation. If the person tries to harm you, ask a responsible adult for help.

 What should you do if someone tries to get you to fight?

What Is a Family?

A **family** is a group of people who are related in some way. Families can be different sizes. They can be made up of different family members.

- A *nuclear family* is made up of a husband and a wife and one or more children.

- A *single-parent family* has only one parent with one or more children.

- A *blended family* may include a husband and wife who were married before. They each may have children from a previous marriage. They may have children together.

- An *extended family* may include grandparents, aunts, uncles, and cousins. They may even live with you.

Family members care about one another. They love, support, and trust each other. Their **memories**, or things remembered from the past, keep them close for many years.

✓ **Name three types of families.**

On Your Own

ACTIVITY

FOR SCHOOL OR HOME

Write About a Favorite Photo

Find a family photo that has meaning for you. Write two or three sentences telling what memories you have about the photo.

▶ **Families spend time together.**

A59

Family Values

Values are learned in families. **Values** are ideas that guide the way a person acts. Your family influences your values. Suppose nutrition and fitness are important values to your parents or guardian. They might teach which foods are healthful. They might also teach you to be physically active.

Your parents or guardian teach you values. They want you to become loving and responsible. They want you to learn to care for yourself and others. They want you to be the best person you can be.

► You learn values when you share time working with your family.

Ways to Be a Responsible Family Member

Being a responsible family member takes practice. Here's what you can do.

- **Show respect.** Act in ways that show respect. Give family members privacy when they need it. Do not say mean things or talk back.

- **Be responsible.** Other family members can depend on you when you are responsible. Try to do your chores on time and follow family guidelines.

- **Be understanding.** Care about how your actions affect other family members. Turn down your music when a family member has a headache. Help a younger brother or sister with his or her homework.

- **Use self-control.** *Self-control* is being able to stop doing something you should not do. Follow family guidelines and stick to family values.

What are family values?

ACTIVITY LIFE SKILLS

CRITICAL THINKING

Access Health Facts, Products, and Services

Your mother has a migraine headache. You want to show her you care. Use this activity to access health facts, products, and services.

1. **Identify when you might need health facts, products, and services.** Why might you need health facts?

2. **Identify where you might find health facts, products, and services.** Talk with a parent or guardian about migraine headaches. Where might you look to find information about migraine headaches?

3. **Find the health facts, products, and services you need.** Find all the health facts you can about migraine headaches. What can you do to help ease your mother's pain? Write down the facts.

4. **Evaluate the health facts, products, and services.** Review with your parents or guardian the health facts you've found. Is the information helpful? How might you use it in the future?

Changes in Families

Every family changes. A baby may be born. A child may be *adopted* or taken into the family from another family. Parents may separate, divorce, and remarry. A family may move. A family member may be away in the military. A loved one may become ill. A family member may die.

Adjusting to Change

Family changes are not always easy. But families can find healthful ways to adjust.

- **Ask others for support.** Let family members know what you think. Share how you feel. Ask your family for help.

- **Offer help.** Help others with their chores. Take time to talk.

- **Ask questions.** Adults in your family can answer your questions. They can explain what to expect when things change.

- **Manage stress.** Follow the steps to manage stress. Get plenty of rest and sleep. Eat healthful foods.

- **Show kindness to other family members.** Acts of kindness make everyone feel better.

▲ A new baby takes much of a family's time. How could you help out?

Adjusting to Death

One of the hardest family changes to adjust to is death. A family member may die. A family pet may die. There is a loss. You may feel great sadness. You may feel angry. You may feel grief. *Grief* is feeling very sad. If you feel grief, talk to a parent or guardian. Tell how you feel. Express your emotion healthfully.

There are healthful ways to adjust to death. Share your feelings with your parents, guardian, or other family members. Remember that it is okay to feel sad or angry. Express your feelings in healthful ways. Use I-messages if you are angry. Share your memories with others.

Day Care Teacher

Day care teachers work with preschool children. They read stories to the children and teach them games. They show them how to get along with others. They talk about how to handle emotions. Day care teachers may also need to help children deal with changes.

LOG ON www.mmhhealth.com Find out more about other health careers.

 What is one of the hardest changes to deal with?

LESSON REVIEW

Review Concepts

1. **Explain** what a family is.

2. **Name** three ways to be a responsible family member.

3. **Tell** three ways you can adjust to family changes.

Critical Thinking

4. **Conclude** Why do you think adjusting to death is so difficult?

5. **LIFE SKILLS** **Access Health Services** If a loved one dies, who might you go to for help?

My Friends

You will learn . . .

- why you need friends.
- ways to make new friends.
- how friends can help each other make responsible decisions.

You may have friends of different ages. You may enjoy talking with an older friend who knows and understands you. You may like playing with a younger friend who can be silly with you. You may like to play games or study with friends your age.

Vocabulary

- **friend**, *A65*
- **disability**, *A67*

Why Do You Need Friends?

A **friend** is a person who likes and supports you. Some people have many friends. Some people may have only one or two close friends. Whatever the case, you need friends for many reasons.

▲ **Friends may share secrets with each other.**

- Friends teach you how to get along with others.

- Friends help you when you feel stress.

- Friends enjoy physical activities with you.

- Friends listen to your ideas and encourage you to try them out.

- Friends protect you from harm. They want what's best for you.

- Friends give you the chance to show that you are a caring person. They spend time with you. They get to know who you are.

Everyone has friends. But not all friends are true friends. How can you tell a true friend from one who isn't? A true friend is responsible and caring. A true friend wants what's best for you.

Write About It!

A True Friend Pick one true friend. Write a short paragraph. Tell what makes this person a true friend. What activities do you share together? What characteristics do you admire in your friend? Why? How would you feel if this person moved away?

 Who is a friend?

Making Friends

Making new friends may seem hard. But if you follow these tips, it might be easier.

- **Think about places you can meet people.** With your parents or guardian, go places where your peers might be. You might join a sports team or a club. There may be children there that you like.

- **When you meet someone you like, make plans together.** Get permission from your parents or guardian first. Ask your parents or guardian to take you to a park where you can play with your new friend.

- **Check out the person. Make sure that he or she is caring and responsible.** It takes time to make a friend. You must spend your time wisely. Do you share the same family values as he or she does? Does this person show respect for you and others?

- **Put time and effort into being a true friend.** To make a true friend you need to be a true friend. Treat the other person the way you want to be treated. Be responsible and caring. Show respect at all times.

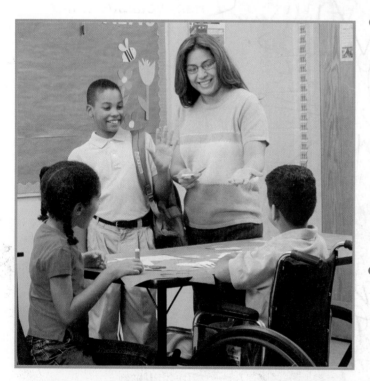

▲ You can make friends with a new student. Make him or her feel welcome.

Friends with Special Needs

You may make friends with someone who has special needs. He or she may have a disability. A **disability** is something that changes a person's ability to do certain tasks.

Suppose that your new friend uses a wheelchair. Having to use a wheelchair causes your friend to have special needs. Your friend might use a ramp to enter a building. Your friend might need someone to hold open a door. Be a good friend to someone who has special needs. Talk about ways to meet the special needs your friend has. Plan activities that your friend can do with you. Your friend in a wheelchair might be able to play basketball. Know that most of your friend's needs are the same as yours.

 What is a disability?

▶ **Students with a disability may enjoy many of the same activities as you.**

Social Studies
L I N K

Make a Poster

Select a country. Find out what health issues the people who live there experience. Make a poster telling what health issues you found. Write suggestions for how the health issue might be handled. Hang your poster in the classroom.

Friends Practice Making Responsible Decisions

True friends help one another make responsible decisions. Here's how.

Guidelines for Making Responsible Decisions™

- Is it healthful?
- Is it safe?
- Does it follow rules and laws?
- Does it show respect for me and others?
- Does it follow family guidelines?
- Does it show good character?

- **Use the *Guidelines for Making Responsible Decisions™*.** The six questions help you know whether a decision is responsible.

- **Do not go along with a friend's wrong decision.** Get away from the situation if it could be harmful.

Taking Responsibility for Health

True friends encourage each other to take responsibility for their health at all times.

- **Make a health behavior contract.** Suppose you and your friend want to get more physical activity. You can make a health behavior contract to help you both reach this goal.

- **Take turns choosing a healthful behavior.** You might choose ice skating one day. Your friend might choose reading. By taking turns you will always do something different.

▲ Friends help each other be the best that they can be.

 What should you do if a friend is about to make a wrong decision?

Make Responsible Decisions

You have made a new friend. You plan to ride bikes after school. You aren't sure where to ride. What should you do?

1 **Identify your choices. Check them out with your parent or trusted adult.** You could ride near your house. Where else might you ride bikes?

2 **Evaluate each choice. Use the *Guidelines for Making Responsible Decisions*™.** Answer the questions for each choice.

3 **Identify the responsible decision. Check this out with your parent or trusted adult.** Explain why your decision is responsible.

4 **Evaluate your decision.** Explain what might happen if you make the decision. Analyze your decision. Is it responsible? If not, go back to step 3.

LESSON REVIEW

Review Concepts

1. **Name** three reasons you need friends.

2. **Tell** three ways to make friends.

3. **Identify** three ways you can make responsible decisions with friends.

Critical Thinking

4. **Analyze** When might you need to make a new friend?

5. **LIFE SKILLS** **Make Responsible Decisions** You are skateboarding with a friend. She skates down a busy street. What should you do?

CHAPTER 2 REVIEW

Use Vocabulary

body language, *A47*

conflict, *A51*

disability, *A67*

friend, *A65*

memories, *A59*

peer, *A54*

relationship, *A45*

value, *A60*

Choose the correct term from the list to complete each sentence.

1. A disagreement is a(n) __?__.
2. Someone who is the same age as you is a(n) __?__.
3. The way you move your body to communicate is __?__.
4. A person who likes and supports you is a(n) __?__.
5. Things that you remember from your past are __?__.
6. A connection you have with another person is a(n) __?__.
7. Something that changes a person's ability to do certain tasks is a(n) __?__.
8. A(n) __?__ is an idea that guides the way a person acts.

Review Concepts

Answer each question in complete sentences.

9. What is peer pressure?
10. What is the first step to use to resolve conflict?
11. What is a value?
12. What is the meaning of the word *communicate*?
13. What is a disability?

Reading Comprehension

Answer each question in complete sentences.

- **Show good character.** Do not ask others to do anything wrong. Do not ask friends to break school rules. Encourage your friends to show good character.

- **Follow family guidelines.** Show respect for your *family guidelines*, or rules set by parents or guardians that tell you how to act. Do not break rules. Don't do something you know you shouldn't do.

14. Why shouldn't you ask others to do something wrong?
15. What are family guidelines?

Critical Thinking/Problem Solving

Answer each question in complete sentences.

Analyze Concepts

16. You're at home watching your favorite television program. Your mom comes home from the grocery store. What might you do to show you care? Explain how your actions show caring.

17. You are playing baseball. You notice that a teammate is cheating. What might you do?

18. At lunch two of your friends are gossiping about another friend. You don't participate. Your friends become angry with you. Did you do the right thing? Why or why not?

19. Why might a peer bully other people?

20. List the four steps in making responsible decisions. How might these steps help you decide if a friend is a true friend?

Practice Life Skills

21. Resolve Conflicts A friend gets angry with you because you did not play with her during recess. How could you resolve this conflict?

22. Make Responsible Decisions Your younger brother wants to play football with you and your friends. You are worried that he may get injured. He is so much smaller than everyone else. Use the *Guidelines for Making Responsible Decisions*™ to help you make a responsible decision.

Read Graphics

Complete the chart below by listing the type of family for each description.

Types of Families	
23.	One parent with two children
24.	Two parents, one child, a grandparent, and an uncle
25.	Two parents and three children
26.	Two parents who were married before with children of their own. One new baby

 LOG ON www.mmhhealth.com
Find out more about family and social health.

Effective Communication

Write a Letter

Your family has moved to a new city. You left your best friend behind. Write a letter to your friend telling how you feel. Include in your letter ways the two of you can stay in touch.

Self-Directed Learning

Make a Family Time Line

Bring in family photos to show how your family has changed. For each photo, write a caption telling about the picture.

Critical Thinking and Problem Solving

Write a Skit

Work with a partner and write a skit about family guidelines. For each rule you include, determine what might happen if it is broken. Perform the skit for your class.

Responsible Citizenship

Adopt a Senior Citizen

Plan a class project to adopt a group of senior citizens. Make cookies or write notes and send them to the group. Think of other activities you might be able to do with your new friends.

Adopt a Senior

UNIT B

Growth and Nutrition

CHAPTER 3

Growth and Development, *B2*

CHAPTER 4

Nutrition, *B36*

CHAPTER 3
Growth and Development

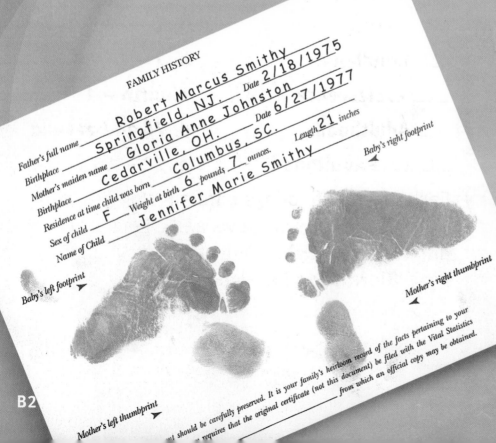

FAMILY HISTORY

Father's full name   Robert Marcus Smithy

Birthplace   Springfield, NJ.   Date 2/18/1975

Mother's maiden name   Gloria Anne Johnston

Birthplace   Cedarville, OH.   Date 6/27/1977

Residence at time child was born   Columbus, SC.

Sex of child   F   Weight at birth 6 pounds 7 ounces.   Length 21 inches

Name of Child   Jennifer Marie Smithy

Baby's right footprint

Baby's left footprint

Mother's right thumbprint

Mother's left thumbprint

...al should be carefully preserved. It is your family's heirloom record of the facts pertaining to your ... requires that the original certificate (not this document) be filed with the Vital Statistics from which an official copy may be obtained.

What Do You Know?

We give names to different times in a person's life. Look at the list below. See if you can match the age span to the correct time of life.

___?___ **Infancy**

___?___ **Childhood**

___?___ **Adolescence**

___?___ **Adulthood**

___?___ **Late Adulthood**

a. 18 – 70

b. 1 – 12

c. birth – 1

d. 70 and beyond

e. 12 – 18

Each time of life brings different changes to your body. Everyone grows and changes at different rates. What time of life are you in? Read **Growth and Development** to find out.

LOG ON www.mmhhealth.com
Find out more about growth and development.

Growing and Changing

- about the stages of the life cycle.
- about signs that show your body is changing.
- how your body grows.

Vocabulary

- **life cycle**, *B5*
- **adolescence**, *B5*
- **puberty**, *B6*
- **cell**, *B8*
- **tissue**, *B8*
- **body system**, *B8*

From the day you were born, you have been growing and changing. You have grown taller. You have become stronger. You look older. As you age, you will continue to grow and change in many exciting ways.

4 F

3 F

The Life Cycle

The stages of life from birth to death make up the **life cycle**.

Your stage of the life cycle is childhood. There are five main stages in the human life cycle. They are listed in the chart below.

Stages of the Life Cycle

Stage	Description
Infancy (IN•fuhn•see)	The stage from birth to age one. You grew quickly, learned to roll over, sit up, and reach for objects.
Childhood	The stage from age 1 to age 12. During childhood you learn to manage your emotions, to solve problems, and to get along with others.
Adolescence (ad•uh•LES•uhns)	The stage from age 12 to age 18. You enter puberty and grow into an adult.
Adulthood	The longest stage of the life cycle, from age 18 to age 70. Young adults may live on their own, go to college, find a job, get married, and have a family.
Late adulthood	The stage from age 70 and beyond. Older adults may retire from their jobs, keep working, or volunteer. They experience physical and mental changes as their bodies age.

 What are the five stages of the human life cycle?

Make a Time Line
Think of all of the major changes in your life. Then make a time line. Begin with the date of your birth. End with your last birthday. Mark the times when your body grew or changed the most. Include important events. Tell about each event, using complete sentences.

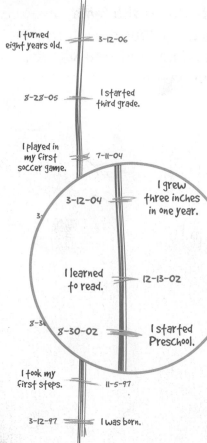

I turned eight years old. ═ 3-12-06

8-28-05 ═ I started third grade.

I played in my first soccer game. ═ 7-11-04

3-12-04 ═ I grew three inches in one year.

3-

I learned to read. ═ 12-13-02

8-3

8-30-02 ═ I started Preschool.

I took my first steps. ═ 11-5-97

3-12-97 ═ I was born.

Your Growing, Changing Body

As you get older, you grow taller and gain weight. Growth isn't steady, though. It often happens in *spurts*, or all of a sudden.

Growth also takes place at different rates. Your shortest classmate today might be the tallest next year. You may have some primary and some permanent teeth. Some of your classmates might have all their permanent teeth.

As your body changes, it enters puberty. **Puberty** (PYEW•buhr•tee) is the time when the body becomes able to reproduce. Girls enter puberty between ages 10 and 12. Boys enter puberty around age 12 or 13. During puberty, you will go through a big growth spurt. Your body will start to look like an adult's body.

▲ **As you grow, you learn new things.**

Growing Up

Along with physical changes, growing up brings mental and emotional changes. It brings family and social changes, too.

Mental and Emotional As you age, you will take on more and more responsibility for yourself. You will develop many different skills and interests. You will learn how to manage your emotions.

Family and Social The activities you enjoy might change. You might have enjoyed splashing around in the pool when you were five. Now you may enjoy swimming laps or diving with friends. Today, you probably spend more time with family than with friends. When you're older, you may spend more time with friends than with family.

 What is puberty?

▶ These girls are the same age. Growth occurs at different rates for everyone.

ACTIVITY

LIFE SKILLS

CRITICAL THINKING

Access Health Facts, Products, and Services

Your friend feels terrible. She is much shorter than her classmates. What can you do to help your friend? Work with a partner. Role-play to help your friend.

1. **Identify when you might need health facts, products, and services.** What kind of information might your friend need? Make a list of your ideas.

2. **Identify where you might find health facts, products, and services.** What sources might you use?

3. **Find the health facts, products, and services you need.** Visit the library to find reliable sources or use your textbook.

4. **Evaluate the health facts, products, and services.** Was the information you found helpful? How will you use the information to help your friend?

Your Body Systems

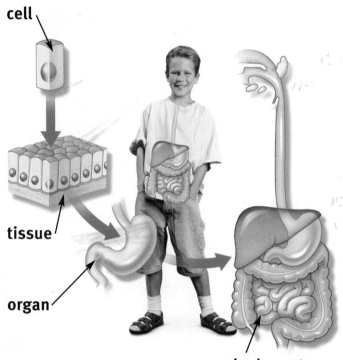

cell

tissue

organ

body system

▲ Body systems start with cells. What do tissues form?

A **cell** is the smallest living part of the body. Some of the cells your body has are skin cells, blood cells, and bone cells. Cells are the building blocks of your body.

Some cells in your body work together. Cells that work together form a **tissue** (TI•shew). Your muscles are made up of tissue. Tissue works together to form *organs*. Your heart is an organ.

A **body system** is a group of organs that work together to do a job. Your heart, blood, and blood vessels form the circulatory system.

Major Body Systems

Body System and Function	Made Up of
Skeletal—Gives body support and shape; helps the body move	Bones, including the skull, ribs, vertebrae, and femurs
Muscular—Helps the body move; works together with bones	Muscles, including arm, thigh, and calf muscles
Circulatory—Moves blood through the body	Heart, arteries, veins
Respiratory—Helps the body use the air you breathe	Nose, throat, windpipe, lungs
Digestive—Helps the body use food to make energy	Salivary glands, stomach, small intestine, large intestine
Nervous—Controls all body actions	Brain, spinal cord, nerves, sense organs (eyes, ears, nose, mouth, skin)

Caring for Body Systems

You can help your body systems grow and stay healthy.

- **Eat healthful foods.** Eat plenty of fruits, vegetables, and fiber, such as whole-wheat bread and brown rice. Limit the amount of fatty foods you eat.

- **Get plenty of physical activity.** Walk, run, bike, skate, or swim. Play sports. Physical activity helps your body systems work better.

 Name two actions you can take to care for your body systems.

▶ **To run, you use five body systems: nervous, circulatory, muscular, skeletal, and respiratory.**

LESSON REVIEW

Review Concepts

1. **Tell** what the life cycle is.

2. **List** four signs that you are growing.

3. **Explain** how your body grows.

Critical Thinking

4. **Compare** Choose two body systems from the chart on page B8. Tell how they are alike and different.

5. **Analyze** Joe exercises everyday. He also eats lots of candy and fried foods. Is Joe taking care of his body systems correctly?

6. **LIFE SKILLS** **Access Health Facts, Products, and Services** You've been feeling pain in your bones. You haven't been injured. You don't know what's causing the pain. What can you do?

Your Muscles and Bones

You will learn . . .

- about the way your muscles work.
- what your bones do.
- ways to care for muscles and bones.

Vocabulary

- **muscle**, *B11*
- **skeleton**, *B12*
- **joint**, *B13*

Your muscles help you move. Your bones support your weight and build. It takes healthy muscles and bones to allow your body to walk, run, and do cartwheels.

How Your Muscles Work

Your *muscular* (MUHS•kyuh•luhr) *system* is a body system made up of muscles. A **muscle** (MUH•suhl) is a type of tissue made of strong fibers. Muscles let your body move. Some muscles are attached to bones. They work in pairs to help you move.

Your arm muscles help you perform many tasks. They help you lift objects and carry things. Your arm muscles help you pull open a door. They help you push your chair toward the table. Your arm muscles help you throw and catch a ball.

Your thigh muscles are in your upper legs. Your thigh muscles move your leg forward and backward. This movement takes place at the hip and knee. These muscles help you walk and run.

Your calf muscles are in the back of your lower leg. Your calf muscles bend your leg at the ankle. You need strong calf muscles to play many sports. You use calf muscles when you run, walk, ski, skate, and bike.

 Name three actions that your leg muscles perform.

▲ All the muscles in your body make up your muscular system. What do muscles do?

How Your Bones Work

skull

elbow joint

ribs

vertebrae

femurs

knee joint

Your bones form your *skeletal system*. The **skeleton** (SKE•luh•tuhn) is the framework of your bones. The skeleton supports the body. It also protects the soft tissues inside the body. Your skeleton gives your body its shape. With your muscles, your skeleton helps you move.

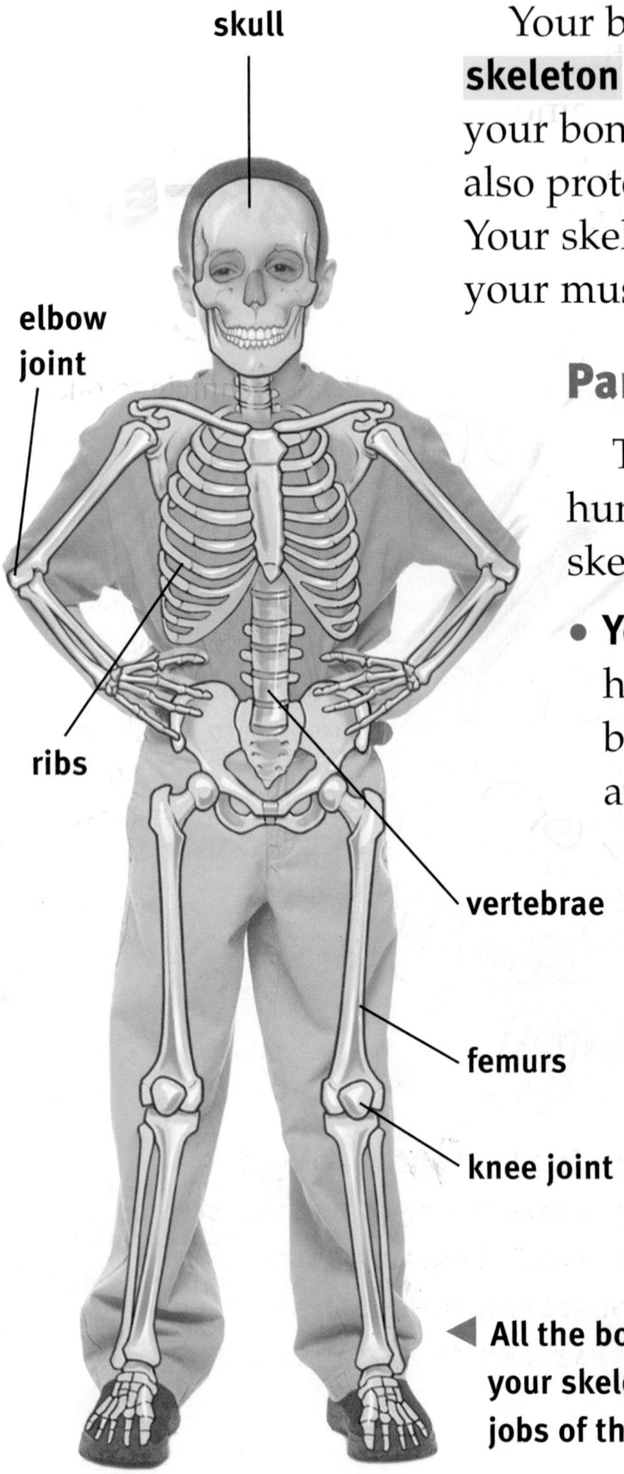

Parts of the Skeleton

There are more than 200 bones in the human body. These bones form your skeleton.

- **Your skull** is made of the bones in your head and face. There are eight different bones in your skull. Your skull covers and protects your brain.

◀ All the bones in your body make up your skeletal system. What are the jobs of the skeletal system?

- **Your ribs** are the bones that cover and protect your heart and lungs. Ribs also help support your shoulders and arms. Your ribs are arranged in pairs.

- **Your vertebrae** (VUR•tuh•bree) are the twenty-six bones that make up your spine, or backbone. Your spine supports your body and head. Your vertebrae let you bend in many directions.

- **Your femurs** (FEE•muhrz) are your thigh bones. They are the largest and strongest bones in your body.

Your Joints

A **joint** is the place where two or more bones meet. Your joints help you bend and move. The joint at your knee helps you bend your leg. The joint at your elbow helps you bend your arm. Different joints let your body move in different ways.

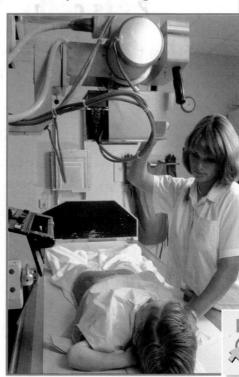

▲ Using X rays is a kind of *technology.* Technology means "using ideas from science to do something." X rays are a kind of light that you cannot see. We cannot *see* X rays, but we can *use* them to take pictures.

 What are two jobs of the skeleton?

Keeping Muscles and Bones Healthy

Your body depends on strong muscles and bones. They support your body and protect your organs. Caring for your muscles and bones will make them stronger.

Caring for Your Muscles

There are a number of ways you can care for your muscles.

- **Use your muscles.** Regular physical activity makes muscles thicker and stronger. Strong muscles can help you lift, pull, push, and kick.

- **Stretch your muscles.** Stretching exercises keep your muscles flexible. *Flexibility* (flek•suh•BI•luh•tee) means being able to bend and move easily. Stretch your muscles before and after physical activity.

- **Eat foods with calcium and magnesium.** Calcium and magnesium help muscles work well. Choose milk, cheese, yogurt, green leafy vegetables, nuts, beans, cereals, breads, and seafood.

▶ These foods are healthful for your muscles. Which of these foods contain calcium? Which ones contain magnesium?

B14

Caring for Your Bones

There are ways to care for your bones, too.

- **Choose weight-bearing activities.** Running, walking, and dancing are good examples of *weight-bearing activities*.

- **Eat foods with calcium, phosphorus, and vitamin D.** These substances make your bones strong.

- **Sit and stand straight.** *Posture* (POS•chuhr) is the way you hold your body as you sit, stand, and move. When you have good posture, you sit and stand straight.

 What are two ways to keep muscles healthy?

ACTIVITY — LIFE SKILLS / CRITICAL THINKING

Set Health Goals

You want your friends to protect their muscles and bones. Work with a partner to create a poster.

1. **Write the health goal you want to set.** I will get plenty of exercise.

2. **Explain how your goal might affect your health.** How will physical activity protect muscles and bones?

3. **Describe a plan you will follow to reach your goal. Keep track of your progress.** Tell who can help you reach this goal—a teacher, a school nurse, a doctor, or a coach. Include this information on your poster. Develop a Health Behavior Contract.

4. **Evaluate how your plan worked.** What might you do if your plan fails? Include this information on your poster. Share your poster with your classmates.

LESSON REVIEW

Review Concepts

1. **Name** four actions your arm muscles perform.

2. **Identify** the parts of the skeleton.

3. **Tell** three ways you can care for your bones and muscles.

Critical Thinking

4. **Assess** Pretend that you cannot use your elbow joint. Assess how this would affect how you move.

5. **LIFE SKILLS** **Set Health Goals** You want to do physical activities that will get your heart working faster. What should you do?

Your Heart and Lungs

You will learn . . .

- about the circulatory system.
- about the respiratory system.
- how to care for your heart and lungs.

Vocabulary

- **heart**, *B17*
- **oxygen**, *B18*
- **carbon dioxide**, *B18*
- **lungs**, *B18*

When you exercise, you may become tired. Your face may look red. You may sweat. This is because exercise makes your heart and lungs work harder. Exercise keeps your heart and lungs strong and healthy.

The Circulatory System

The heart, blood, and blood vessels are parts of your *circulatory system*. Your **heart** is an organ that pumps blood into your blood vessels with each heartbeat. It rests between each heartbeat. Your *blood vessels* are tubes that carry blood throughout your body.

Your body has two main types of blood vessels: arteries and veins. Your *arteries* (AHR•tuh•reez) carry blood away from your heart. They move oxygen in the blood and substances to body cells.

Your *veins* bring blood back to your heart. Veins have valves. The valves keep blood from flowing backward. Muscles push against the veins to push blood to the heart.

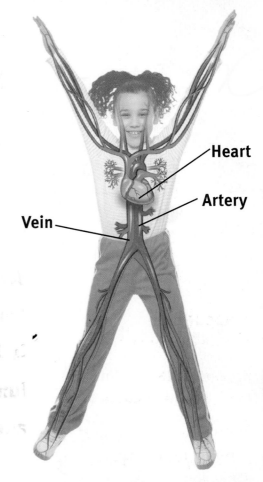

Heart

Artery

Vein

▲ The circulatory system is made up of organs that move blood throughout your body.

✓ What are arteries?

ACTIVITY

Math LINK

Find Your Pulse

With the help of an adult, find your pulse on your wrist. Your pulse is the pressure you feel in your arteries when the aortic valve opens and closes in your heart. You can feel your pulse each time your heart beats. Count the number of pulses you feel in one minute. What number did you count? If your heart beats 75 times per minute, how many times does it beat in one hour? In one day?

The Respiratory System

Your *respiratory* (RES•puhr•uh•tor•ee) system moves oxygen into your body. It releases carbon dioxide from the body. **Oxygen** (OK•si•juhn) is a gas that you need to live. **Carbon dioxide** (KAHR•buhn•digh•OK•sighd) is a gas, too, but it is a waste product of your cells.

The respiratory system is made up of the nose, throat, windpipe, and lungs. Your nose draws air into your body. Your throat is the passageway from your mouth to your windpipe. Your windpipe is a tube that goes from your throat to your lungs.

When you breathe in, air passes through your nose and into your body. The air travels from your nose to your throat, down your windpipe, and into your lungs. Your **lungs** are organs that put oxygen into the blood.

 What is carbon dioxide?

ACTIVITY
Consumer Wise

Room Air Cleaners!

People sometimes purchase a room air cleaner to make air healthier to breathe. It removes particles that irritate the lungs. Find out what other types of appliances are used to clean air in a room. You can ask your school nurse or your parents or guardian for help. Share with the class what you find out.

▶ **Health workers can use X rays to take pictures of lungs and other parts inside the body. X rays can help find problems. The earlier a problem is found, the better it can be treated and cured.**

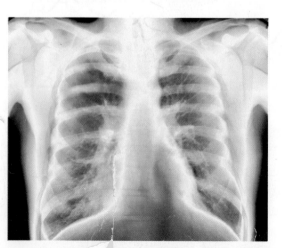

Your respiratory system works with your circulatory system. Blood in your arteries carries the oxygen to body cells. Blood in your veins carries carbon dioxide from body cells to the lungs. When you breathe out, or *exhale*, carbon dioxide leaves your body.

The Respiratory System

nose

throat

windpipe

lung

◀ The respiratory system helps you use the air you breathe.

Be a Health Advocate

Cigarette smoke harms your lungs. Be a health advocate and send a message against smoking. Use this activity to get your message out to others.

1 **Choose a healthful action to communicate.** Communicate why avoiding cigarette smoke is healthy for your body.

2 **Collect information about the action.** Find out how smoking harms the lungs. Record what you find.

3 **Decide how to communicate this information.** Will you make signs or posters? What else could you do?

4 **Communicate your message to others.** Follow through on your healthful action. Make a poster to tell others in your school how to avoid cigarette smoke. In what other ways might you communicate your message to others?

Caring for Your Heart and Lungs

Caring for your heart and lungs will help keep them healthy. Your heart will beat properly. You can inhale deeply, and expand your lungs fully. This will help your body get the amount of oxygen it needs.

Your Heart

You can take action to care for your heart. Here's how.

- **Stay physically active.** Physical activity makes your heart muscle strong. It keeps fat from sticking to arteries. Walking, running, and swimming are healthful activities.

- **Eat low-fat foods.** Low-fat foods are more healthful for your arteries than high-fat foods. Substances in low-fat foods are less likely to stick to artery walls. Drink skim milk. Eat low-fat cheese and avoid fried foods.

- **Say "no" to tobacco.** Using tobacco is harmful to your heart and arteries. Tobacco products contain nicotine. Using tobacco speeds up your heartbeat. The arteries close up. Blood pressure goes up. Stay away from tobacco products.

▼ Swimming makes your heart stronger. When you have a strong heart, you can swim longer.

Your Lungs

You can follow many of the same actions to care for your lungs.

- **Get plenty of physical activity.** Muscles help your lungs work. When your lungs work well, you can move without difficulty.

- **Say "no" to tobacco.** Being smoke-free keeps the respiratory system healthy.

- **Sit and stand straight.** Having good posture helps your lungs work easier. If you slouch, your lungs do not have enough space to expand.

 Name two ways to take care of your lungs.

▲ **Your posture affects how your lungs work. Sitting up straight gives your lungs room to work properly.**

LESSON REVIEW

Review Concepts

1. **Name** the three parts of the circulatory system.

2. **List** the organs that make up the respiratory system.

3. **Tell** three ways to care for your heart.

Critical Thinking

4. **Explain** Why does it take both the respiratory system and the circulatory system to get oxygen to all parts of the body?

5. **LIFE SKILLS** **Be a Health Advocate** You want to let classmates know how they can keep their heart and lungs strong. How might you communicate this message?

Your Digestive System

You will learn . . .

- how your digestive system works.
- how to care for the digestive system.

Vocabulary

- **digestion**, *B23*

The food you eat supplies your body with energy. The body system that allows this to happen is the digestive system. The digestive system breaks food down into a form the body can use.

How the Digestive System Works

Digestion (di•JES•chuhn) is the process of changing food into a form your body can use. This process takes place in your *digestive* (digh•JES•tiv) *system*. Your *salivary* (SA•luh•vayr•ee) *glands* make saliva. *Saliva* (suh•LIGH•vuh) is a liquid in your mouth that softens food. As you chew, your teeth break the softened food into small pieces. Food that is broken down into small pieces is easier to swallow. The softened food moves down a tube to your stomach.

Your stomach releases juices that break down food even more. There food is changed into a thick paste. The paste then moves into your small intestine.

Your small intestine finishes changing food into a form your body cells can use.

Your large intestine moves solid waste out of the body. Solid waste is food that cannot be digested.

 What happens to food in the stomach?

Health Online

Water Works

Research the role of water in digestion. Use the e-journal writing tool to write a report. Visit **www.mmhhealth.com** and click on e-Journal.

The Digestive System

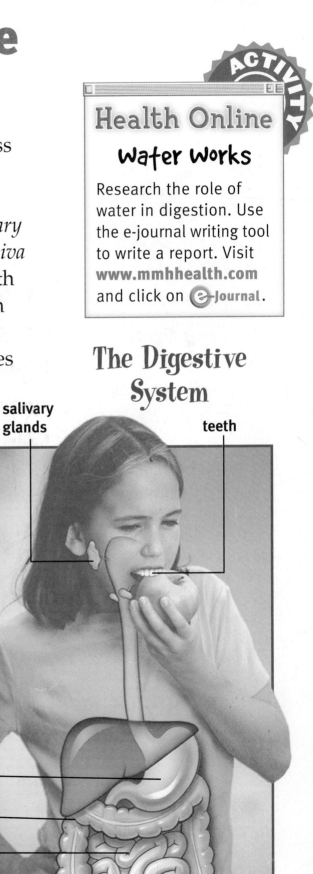

salivary glands

teeth

stomach

large intestine

small intestine

Caring for Your Digestive System

ACTIVITY

On Your Own
FOR SCHOOL OR HOME

Checking Food for Fiber

Fiber is the part of plants and grains that your body cannot break down during digestion. Fruits, vegetables, and grains are foods that contain fiber. Find out how much fiber is in five foods in your house. Look for the Nutrition Facts label on the food package. Which foods have the most fiber per serving? Which ones have the least?

Keep your digestive system healthy by using these tips.

- **Chew your food well.** Chew and eat slowly. This gives saliva a chance to soften food.

- **Eat plenty of fruits, vegetables, and grains.** Eating foods with fiber helps your large intestine move solid waste out of your body. This keeps the large intestine clean.

- **Drink water.** Drinking water helps with digestion. You need at least six to eight glasses of water each day.

- **Get physical activity.** Regular physical activity helps muscles work. Muscles move solid waste through the large intestine and out of the body.

 Which foods help your large intestine move solid waste out of the body?

▶ **You can find out how much fiber is in different foods by looking at the food label on the package.**

Nutrition Facts	
Serving Size 1/2 cup (30g)	
Serving Per Container About 15	
Amount Per Serving	
Calories 60	Calories from Fat 10
	% Daily Value*
Total Fat 1g	1%
Saturated Fat 0g	0%
Trans Fat 0g	
Cholesterol 0mg	0%
Sodium 130mg	5%
Total Carbohydrate 24g	8%
Dietary Fiber 14g	57%
Sugars 0g	
Protein 2g	

Make Responsible Decisions

After school you can choose a snack. Your choices are a candy bar or an apple. What do you do?

1. **Identify your choices. Check them out with your parent or trusted adult.** List the two choices you have.

2. **Evaluate each choice. Use the *Guidelines for Making Responsible Decisions™*.** Answer each question for each choice.

3. **Identify the responsible decision. Check this out with your parent or trusted adult.** What decision are you going to make?

4. **Evaluate your decision.** Explain why it is a responsible decision. Are you happy with your decision? Is it responsible? If not, go back to step three.

Guidelines for Making Responsible Decisions™

- **Is it healthful?**
- **Is it safe?**
- **Does it follow rules and laws?**
- **Does it show respect for myself and others?**
- **Does it follow family guidelines?**
- **Does it show good character?**

LESSON REVIEW

Review Concepts

1. **Describe** the steps involved in the digestive system.

2. **List** three actions you can take to care for your digestive system.

3. **Define** the term digestion.

Critical Thinking

4. **Connect** How might the digestive system and the circulatory system work together?

5. **LIFE SKILLS** **Make Responsible Decisions** You are thirsty after shooting free throws. Your friend's mom allows you to choose from her ice chest. She has soda pop and bottled water. Which should you choose?

Your Senses and Nervous System

You will learn . . .

- about the five sense organs.
- what the nervous system does.
- how to care for the nervous system.

Vocabulary

- **nerve cell**, *B27*
- **brain**, *B28*
- **spinal cord**, *B29*

You get information about the world from your senses. Look around you. What do you see? Listen. What do you hear? Breathe. What do you smell? You can do all of this because of your nervous system.

The Five Sense Organs

Your body collects information using *sense organs*. **Nerve cells** carry messages from these sense organs to your brain.

All five sense organs work together. Your nerve cells work with your sense organs to carry information to your brain. Your brain interprets the information. It tells other parts of your body what to do.

Sense Organ	Description
Ears	Nerve cells inside your ears collect information about sounds and noises.
Eyes	A nerve at the back of your eyeball sends information about what objects look like to the brain.
Skin	Nerve cells deep in your skin collect information about how objects feel. They also sense cold, heat, pain, and touch.
Tongue	*Taste buds* on your tongue tell you whether something is sweet, sour, salty, or bitter.
Nose	Nerve cells inside the nose sense odors. These cells send the information to the brain.

 What are the five sense organs?

ACTIVITY

Art
L I N K

Close Your Eyes and Draw!

Collect a piece of white paper and a pencil. While sitting at your desk, close your eyes and choose an object from the basket that your teacher is passing around the class. Keep your eyes closed and feel the object with your hands. With your eyes closed, try to draw the object that you are touching. Open your eyes. Compare the object you touched with what you drew. How did you do?

Your Nervous System

Your *nervous* (NUHR•vuhs) *system* is made up of organs. They control your body's actions. Nerve cells in these organs receive and send messages to all body parts. These messages tell your body what to do.

Your Brain

The **brain** is the organ that receives and sends messages to all body parts. It is made up of nerve cells. Your brain is the main organ of the nervous system.

Your brain directs everything you do. It allows your thoughts, actions, and emotions to work together. Your brain controls voluntary movement. *Voluntary movement* is action you choose to make, such as walking, talking, and eating. Your brain also controls involuntary movement. *Involuntary movement* is action that you don't control. Your heartbeat and breathing are examples of involuntary movement. They occur automatically.

The Nervous System

Brain

Spinal cord

Nerves

▲ Nerves send information to your brain from different parts of your body.

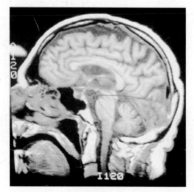

◄ CAT scans are a kind of technology. CAT scans can give pictures of a person's brain. They can help find any problems. The earlier a problem is found, the better it can be treated and cured.

Your Nerves

Nerves are long, thin groups of cells in your body. Some nerves carry messages from your sense organs to your brain. Suppose that a CD is playing. The nerve cells in your ears send a message to the hearing center in your brain. You hear the music.

Your Spinal Cord

The **spinal cord** is a long column of nerve cells. It sends messages to and from your brain. Your spinal cord allows messages to travel between your brain and other parts of your body. Your spinal cord is surrounded by your spine.

✓ **What are the main parts of the nervous system?**

Write About It!

Your Sense Organs at Work Think of a place. It might be the beach, your bedroom, or the school cafeteria. List all the things you might see, smell, hear, taste, and feel in the place you chose. Then write a paragraph describing how this information is sent to your brain.

▶ **Your nervous system helps you understand information and respond to it.**

BUILD
Character

Analyze Your Actions

Responsibility Think about everything you do in a day. Make a list of at least 10 actions that use your nervous system. Next to each action, list a way you can take responsibility for the health of your nervous system. You need a healthy brain to do all the things you do every day. That's why it's important to take care of your nervous system.

Caring for Your Nervous System

Here's how you can take care of your nervous system.

- **Wear your seat belt while riding in a car.** Wearing a seat belt protects your brain and spinal cord if you are in a car crash.

- **Say "no" to drugs.** Being drug-free helps protect nerve cells. Alcohol is a depressant drug. It slows down the action of nerve cells. Marijuana (mar•uh•WAH•nuh) is a harmful drug. It changes how your brain senses the world. Stay away from all illegal or harmful drugs.

- **Wear a helmet.** Wearing a helmet for certain physical activities protects your brain from injury. Wear a helmet when you ride your bike or scooter or skate. Many sports have rules that require players to wear a helmet. Baseball, football, and hockey are examples.

Protect Yourself from Harmful Fumes

Always protect yourself when you are around any fumes. Fumes are gasses given off by paints and glue.

- Wear a special mask when around cleaners, paints, or glues. A mask keeps you safe from breathing fumes.

- Open a window when near fumes. An open window airs out the room.

 What are two ways to protect yourself from fumes?

ACTIVITY LIFE SKILLS · CRITICAL THINKING

Use Communication Skills

Your friend lends you her scooter. You really want to take a turn. You don't have a helmet. Work with a partner. Write a skit to tell what you can do.

1. **Choose the best way to communicate.** How will you communicate with your friend?

2. **Send a clear message. Be polite.** Explain why you need a helmet. Use I-messages.

3. **Listen to each other.** Role-play using the message you wrote.

4. **Make sure you understand each other.** Tell what you heard. Then switch roles and do the activity again.

LESSON REVIEW

Review Concepts

1. **Explain** how nerve cells work with sense organs.

2. **Tell** what the nervous system does.

3. **Explain** why it's important to wear a helmet when doing certain physical activities. Give an example of an activity where you would wear a helmet.

Critical Thinking

4. **Apply** As you arrive home from school, your dog greets you. How might you react? How do your brain and nerves work when you react?

5. **LIFE SKILLS Use Communication Skills** Your older brother is driving you to school. He doesn't want to wear his safety belt. He says he doesn't need to because your school is so close by. What do you say?

Learning LIFE SKILLS

Manage Stress

Problem Over the weekend, Alice broke her arm. Now she is worried. How will she get her schoolwork done. Alice may be feeling stress.

Solution Alice can manage her stress. Use the four steps on the next page to find out how.

Learn This Life Skill

Follow these four steps to help manage stress.
The Foldables™ can help you.

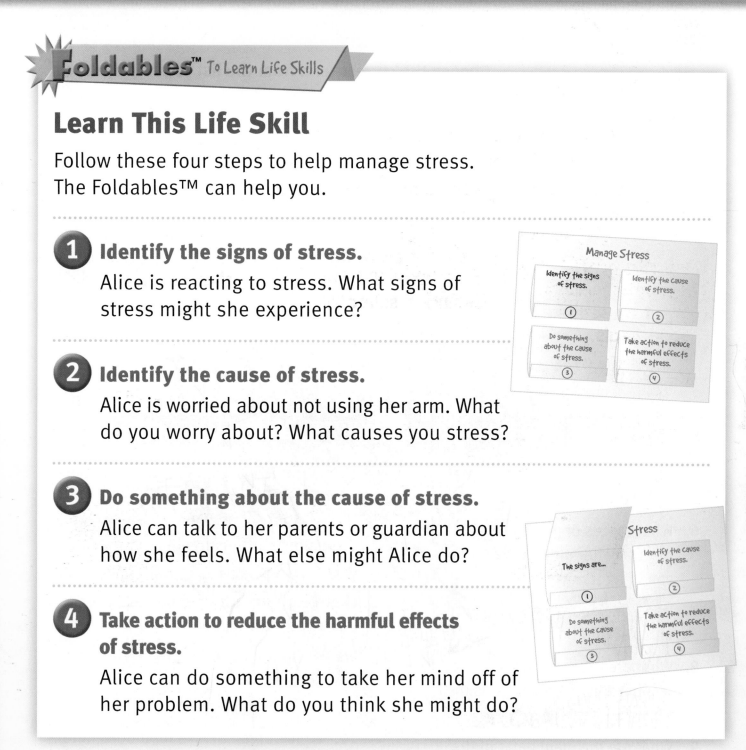

1 **Identify the signs of stress.**

Alice is reacting to stress. What signs of stress might she experience?

2 **Identify the cause of stress.**

Alice is worried about not using her arm. What do you worry about? What causes you stress?

3 **Do something about the cause of stress.**

Alice can talk to her parents or guardian about how she feels. What else might Alice do?

4 **Take action to reduce the harmful effects of stress.**

Alice can do something to take her mind off of her problem. What do you think she might do?

Practice This Life Skill

Work with a group of classmates. Think of a situation that might cause stress. Use the four steps above and write a skit about managing stress. Role-play the skit in your group.

CHAPTER 3 REVIEW

Use Vocabulary

Choose the correct term from the list to complete each sentence.

body system, *B8*

joint, *B13*

lungs, *B18*

muscle, *B11*

spinal cord, *B29*

1. The column of nerve cells that carry messages to and from the brain is called the __?__.

2. A(n) __?__ is a place where two or more bones meet.

3. Organs that put oxygen into the blood and take out carbon dioxide are __?__.

4. A(n) __?__ is a group of organs that work together to do a certain job.

5. A tissue that allows your body to move is called __?__.

Review Concepts

Answer each question in complete sentences.

6. What stages of growth do people go through after birth? Which stage are you in right now?

7. How can you take care of your muscles and bones?

8. What are the main parts of the respiratory system? What is the function of each part?

9. What are the main parts of the circulatory system? What is the function of each part?

10. List the five sense organs. What is the main job of sense organs?

Reading Comprehension

Your stomach is an organ that releases juices that break down food. Food is changed into a thick paste. The paste then moves into your small intestine.

Your small intestine is the organ that changes food into substances your body cells can use.

Your large intestine is the organ that moves solid waste, or food that cannot be digested, out of the body.

11. Which organ breaks food down into a paste?

12. Explain the function of the small intestine.

13. What happens to solid waste?

Critical Thinking/Problem Solving

Answer each question in complete sentences.

Analyze Concepts

14. Your older sister is 14. Four months ago she was 4 feet 9 inches tall. Now she is 5 feet tall. What caused her to grow so quickly?

15. After a cast is removed, how can you make a bone stronger?

16. You and your friends have been running very fast. You become tired more quickly than your friends. What can you do about it?

17. What might happen if you don't chew your food well?

18. You see the ball. You raise your foot to kick it. What organ helps you coordinate these actions?

Practice Life Skills

19. **Manage Stress** Keep a weekly log of stressful situations you experience. Describe how you felt under stress.

20. **Make Responsible Decisions** You are at a friend's house. He suggests that you jump off the top bunk of his bed onto the floor. What should you do? Use the *Guidelines for Making Responsible Decisions*™ to help you decide.

Read Graphics

The graph compares lung cancer cases with the number of cigarettes smoked per day. Use the graph to answer questions 21–23.

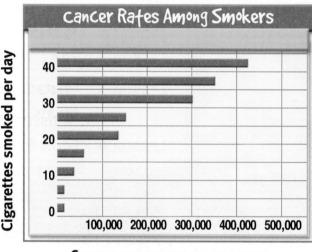

Cancer cases per 100,000 men
Source: American Cancer Society

21. How many cancer cases occur when 30 cigarettes are smoked per day?

22. How many cancer cases occur when 40 cigarettes are smoked per day?

23. How many more cancer cases occur when 40 cigarettes are smoked per day instead of 30?

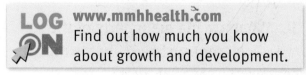

www.mmhhealth.com
Find out how much you know about growth and development.

CHAPTER 4

Nutrition

What Do You Know?

Are you eating enough of the foods you need each day? Do you know what foods your body needs to stay healthy? Read each statement. Answer **yes** or **no**.

__?__ Meals should include fruits and vegetables.

__?__ Eating too much sugary food is not healthful.

__?__ Food labels tell how much fat is in a serving of food.

__?__ Food gives your body energy.

Did you answer **yes** to all the questions? If so, you are off to a good start. Read **Nutrition** to find out more.

 LOG ON www.mmhhealth.com
Find out more about nutrition.

Why You Need Food

You will learn . . .

- what nutrients your body needs.
- what foods are in the food groups.
- how to use MyPyramid to make healthful food choices.

Vocabulary

- **energy**, *B39*
- **diet**, *B39*
- **nutrient**, *B39*
- **vitamins**, *B39*
- **MyPyramid**, *B40*

To play a game of catch, you need energy. In fact, you need energy to do everything! Where do you get this energy? You get energy from food.

Your Body Needs Nutrients

Energy is the ability to do work. You get the energy your body needs from your **diet**, or the foods and drinks you digest. Foods and drinks contain nutrients. A **nutrient** (NEW•tree•uhnt) is a material in a food or drink that is used by the body. You need six kinds of nutrients. Some help you grow. Some give you energy. Others help your body work well. A healthful diet gives you all the nutrients you need.

▼ Pasta is a source of carbohydrates.

The Six Main Nutrients	Food and Drink Sources
Carbohydrates (kahr•boh•HIGH•drayts) are your body's main energy source.	bread, pasta, rice, cereal, potatoes, fruits, fruit and vegetable juices
Proteins (PROH•teenz) are nutrients used for growth and to repair cells.	meat, fish, eggs, nuts, tofu, dry beans
Fats give you energy. They help cells store and use vitamins.	meat, dairy products, oil, butter
Vitamins (VIGH•tuh•minz) help your body use other nutrients.	vegetables, fruits, juices, meat, dairy products, cereal
Minerals keep your body working properly.	vegetables, fruits, juices, meat, dairy products
Water makes up most of your body. It helps your body use food.	drinking water, milk, fruits, vegetables

▼ Chicken is a source of protein.

▼ Oil is a fat.

 What is a nutrient?

Food Groups

Write a Paragraph You get nutrients from foods and drinks. Make a list showing what foods and drinks you had today. Then write a paragraph about the nutrients in those foods and drinks. Describe how they help your body.

You can use MyPyramid to plan a healthful diet. **MyPyramid** is a guide for healthful eating. It tells you the amounts from each food group your body needs each day. A *serving* is a certain amount of food. A *food group* is made up of foods that give your body the same kinds of nutrients. MyPyramid shows the five food groups.

 What is a food group?

Find your balance between food and fun.

Move at least 60 minutes every day. Walk, dance, bike, rollerblade —it all counts!

Grains
6 oz.

Vegeta
2 1/2 c

Oils

Oils are not a food group, but you need some for good health. Get your oils from fish, nuts, and liquid oils such as corn oil, soybean oil, and canola oil.

Fats and Sugars

Get your facts from the Nutrition Label.

Limit solids and fats. Choose foods low in added sugars and sweetners.

Fruits	Milk	Meat & Beans
1 1/2 cups	3 cups	5 oz.
	(For kids 2–8 yrs, **2 cups**)	

For an 1,800-calorie diet, you need the amounts above from each food group <u>everyday</u>. To find the amounts that are right for you, go to www.MyPyramid.gov

Using MyPyramid

Don't forget to eat the correct amount from each food group every day. Here are examples.

Grains Group

You should eat 6 oz. from this food group daily. Each of these is one oz.

1 slice of bread

1 mini bagel

1 cup ready-to-eat cereal

1/2 cup cooked cereal, rice, or pasta

5 whole wheat crackers

Vegetable Group

You should eat 2 1/2 cups from this food group daily.

Raw, leafy vegetables

Cooked or chopped raw vegetables

Vegetable juice (100%)

Fruit Group

You should eat 1 1/2 cups from this food group daily.

Apples, bananas, or oranges

Chopped, cooked, canned, or mixed fruit

Fruit juice (100%)

Milk Group You should eat 2 cups from this food group daily. Use low-fat or fat-free products.

Milk or yogurt

Natural cheese, like cheddar

Processed cheese

Meat and Beans Group

You should eat 5 oz. of these foods daily.

Cooked lean meat, fish, or poultry

Eggs

Peanut butter

 How many cups of fruit should you eat?

ACTIVITY
LIFE SKILLS

CRITICAL THINKING

Access Health Facts, Products, and Services

Your doctor tells you to get plenty of Vitamin C in your diet. How do you know which foods and drinks have Vitamin C?

1. **Identify when you might need health facts, products, and services.** Find health facts about foods and drinks that contain Vitamin C.

2. **Identify where you might find health facts, products, and services.** Find three sources with health facts about food, drinks, and Vitamin C.

3. **Find the health facts, products, and services you need.** Use all three sources. Write down foods and drinks with Vitamin C.

4. **Evaluate the health facts, products, and services.** Ask your doctor if your facts are correct.

LESSON REVIEW

Review Concepts

1. **Name** the six kinds of nutrients your body needs.

2. **Name** three foods in each of the five food groups.

3. **Tell** how you can use MyPyramid to have a healthful diet.

Critical Thinking

4. **Analyze** Why is it important to eat fruits and vegetables?

5. **LIFE SKILLS Access Health Facts, Products, and Services** You want to learn more about vitamins. What sources could you use?

The Dietary Guidelines

You will learn . . .

- about the Dietary Guidelines.
- how to follow the Dietary Guidelines.
- how to use the Dietary Guidelines to choose snacks that are healthful.

Vocabulary

- **Dietary Guidelines**, *B45*
- **snack**, *B48*

Do you know about the Dietary Guidelines? Do you know how to use them? If so, you can choose healthful meals and snacks.

The Dietary Guidelines

The **Dietary Guidelines** are suggested goals to help you stay healthy. These guidelines help you stay healthy and live longer. They were developed by the U.S. government. There are nine Dietary Guidelines. They list the kinds of foods you should eat. They also list the kinds of foods you should limit or avoid. The Dietary Guidelines explain why you should stay at a healthful weight. They also explain why you should be physically active every day.

 What is the goal of the Dietary Guidelines?

Con$umer Wi$e

Compare Fruit Drinks

Gather a label from a fruit juice and a fruit drink. Read each label. Compare. Which has more sugar? Which product is more healthful?

 CAREERS

Cafeteria Worker

The cafeteria workers at your school help you get the nutrients you need. They may plan meals using MyPyramid and the Dietary Guidelines. Cafeteria workers prepare or cook food. They also serve you food.

 LOG ON www.mmhhealth.com
Find out more about this and other health careers.

How to Follow the Dietary Guidelines

Follow the Dietary Guidelines to stay healthy and live longer. You'll have more energy, too.

1. **Get the calories you need for how active you are.** A *calorie* is a unit used to measure the energy produced by food in the body. Let MyPyramid guide your food choices to get the calories you need.

2. **Stay at a healthful weight.** Being overweight is a health problem. It increases the risk of heart disease, diabetes, and some cancers. Your doctor can tell you how much you should weigh. Eat the right amount of food and get plenty of exercise to maintain a healthful weight.

3. **Be physically active each day.** Physical activity helps you stay at a healthful weight. It also makes your heart, lungs, and muscles strong. It helps you manage stress. You need about 60 minutes of physical activity every day.

4. **Get the nutrients you need from healthful foods.** Eating more fruits, vegetables, whole grains and low-fat or fat-free milk helps you get the vitamins, minerals and fiber that you need.

5. **Choose foods that do not have too much fat.** Limit the meat you eat. When you eat meat, cut the fat off it. Limit pastries, such as donuts, cookies, and cake. Nuts, vegetables, and fish are healthful choices for fats.

6. **Choose foods and drinks that do not have too much sugar.** Candy, cake, and many soft drinks are high in sugar. Eating too much of these foods can make you gain weight. Sugar also can cause tooth decay.

7. **Choose and prepare foods without much salt.** Eating too much salt increases your risk of some diseases. You need less than 1/4 teaspoon of salt each day. Many packaged or canned foods have salt added to them. Try not to add salt to your food. Also eat few salty snacks, such as chips and pretzels.

8. **Keep food safe to eat.** Germs can get into food and make you ill. Wash your hands before you eat or prepare food. Keep dairy foods such as milk cold.

9. **Do not drink alcohol.** Alcohol is a drug. It can harm body organs. It is against the law for people your age to drink alcohol.

write About It!

Stay Healthy, Live Longer Review the Dietary Guidelines listed on pages B46 and B47. Write a summary explaining how the guidelines can help you stay healthy and live longer. Include a plan telling how you can make the Dietary Guidelines a part of your life.

 Why is one goal of the Dietary Guidelines to stay at a healthful weight?

How to Choose Healthful Snacks

A **snack** is food eaten between meals. You can use the Dietary Guidelines to help you choose healthful snacks. Here are some tips.

- **Choose snacks to help you get the right amounts from the food groups.** Use MyPyramid to help you.

- **Choose snacks made from grains.** Whole wheat crackers and cereal are healthful snack choices.

- **Choose fruits and vegetables for snacks.** An apple or orange and carrot sticks help you get the servings needed from the fruit and vegetable food group.

- **Limit snacks that are high in total fat.** These food items include cake, candy, French fries, and hamburgers.

- **Limit snacks that have added sugar.** Avoid soft drinks, fruit drinks with sugar, and candy.

- **Limit snacks with salt.** Choose unsalted pretzels, crackers, and peanuts. Do not add salt to popcorn.

▲ **Fruit makes a healthful snack.**

What is a snack?

Set Health Goals

Are you ready to follow the Dietary Guidelines? Set a goal.

1 **Write the health goal you want to set.** I will eat healthful snacks.

2 **Explain how your goal might affect your health.** Read the Dietary Guidelines again. Suppose you choose snacks that follow the guidelines. List three ways this helps your health.

3 **Describe a plan you will follow to reach your goal. Keep track of your progress.** Make a health behavior contract. Your contract should include a chart with columns for each day of the week. For one week, write down the snacks you eat each day. Tell who can help you—a parent or guardian, a teacher, a school nurse, a school nutritionist.

4 **Evaluate how your plan worked.** After one week, check your chart. Did all the snacks follow the Dietary Guidelines? Did you reach your goal? How could you make your plan better?

LESSON REVIEW

Review Concepts

1. **Tell** what the Dietary Guidelines are.

2. **List** two of the nine Dietary Guidelines.

3. **Identify** two ways to choose healthful snacks.

Critical Thinking

4. **Synthesize** How are the Dietary Guidelines and MyPyramid related?

5. **Practice Healthful Behaviors** You want to limit the salt you eat. How will you use the four steps to practice this healthful behavior?

6. **Set Health Goals** You want to get plenty of physical activity every day. Write a health behavior contract to help you reach this goal.

B49

Choosing Healthful Meals and Snacks

You will learn . . .

- what influences your food choices.
- what facts are found on food labels.
- how to plan a menu for a healthful meal.

Vocabulary

- **ad**, *B51*
- **food label**, *B52*
- **ingredient**, *B52*

You make food choices every day. You might help write your family's shopping list. What influences your food choices? Do you read food labels? Do you clip coupons? Do you compare prices?

Influences on Food Choices

Suppose you are choosing healthful meals and snacks. Why do you choose some foods and drinks and not others? There are probably different reasons for your choices.

- **Personal Preference** You eat many foods because you like the way they taste or smell.

- **Family and Friends** You may eat certain foods because your parents or guardian serve them at meals. Your family's culture may influence food choices. You may have tried some foods served by your friend's parents or guardian when eating at their home.

- **Availability** You may eat a food that is grown in your area. You may choose foods that many people in your community eat.

- **Food Ads** Food companies want you to choose the foods they sell. An **ad** is a notice that tells people about a product. Companies use ads to influence your food choices.

- **Dietary Guidelines** Using the Dietary Guidelines to choose healthful foods and drinks will keep you healthy and help you live longer.

What is an ad?

▶ Family and friends influence your food choices.

Food Labels

Check food labels and prices to help you make wise choices.

Read Food Labels

Most packaged foods have food labels. A **food label** lists the ingredients in the food. It also lists nutrition facts. An **ingredient** (in•GREE•dee•uhnt) is something that goes into making a food or drink. The label lists a food's ingredients in order. The first one listed makes up most of the product. The last one listed is the least ingredient in the product.

► **What ingredient makes up most of this cereal?**

ALMOND CRISP CEREAL

Nutrition Facts
Serving Size 1 cup

Amount/serving		
Calories 130	Fat Calorie 10	

		%
Total Fat 1.0g		2%
Saturated Fat 0g		0%
Cholesterol 0mg		0%
Sodium 310 mg		13%
Potassium 40mg		1%
Total Carb. 30g		10%
Fiber 1g		4%
Sugars 12g		
Protein 2g		

Vitamin A 15%	•	Vitamin C 25%
Calcium 0%	•	Iron 10%
Vitamin D 10%	•	Thiamin 25%
Riboflavin 25%	•	Niacin 25%

* Percent Daily Values (DV) are based on a 2,000 calorie diet.

Ingredients: MILLED CORN, ALMONDS, SUGAR, SALT, HIGH FRUCTOSE CORN SYRUP, IRON, ASCORBIC ACID, FOLIC ACID, VITAMIN B2, NATURAL FLAVORING

ACTIVITY

Math LINK

Compare Packages

The food store is having a sale on canned peas. A 6-ounce can of peas is $0.69. A 15-ounce can of peas is on sale for 1 cent more. How many more ounces of peas do you get for the extra penny you pay?

Nutrition Facts
Serving Size 1 cup (228g)
Serving Per Container 2

Amount Per Serving

Calories 250	Calories from Fat 110

	% Daily Value*
Total Fat 12g	18%
Saturated Fat 3g	15%
Trans Fat 1.5g	
Cholesterol 30mg	10%
Sodium 470mg	20%
Total Carbohydrate 31g	10%
Dietary Fiber 0g	0%
Sugars 5g	
Protein 5g	

Vitamin A	4%
Vitamin C	2%
Calcium	20%
Iron	4%

* Percent Daily Values are based on a 2,000 calorie diet. Your Daily Values may be higher or lower depending on your calorie needs:

	Calories:	2,000	2,500
Total Fat	Less than	65g	80g
Sat Fat	Less than	20g	25g
Cholesterol	Less than	300mg	300mg
Sodium	Less than	2,400 mg	2,400mg
Total Carbohydrate		300g	375g
Dietary Fiber		25g	30g

▲ **This food label for macaroni and cheese gives nutrition information.**

The Nutrition Facts panel is another part of a food label. This panel tells about the nutritional value of the food. It tells you how much of the food makes up a serving. It also tells how many nutrients are in one serving.

Compare Prices

You can also compare prices to make your choice. If the food labels are similar, but one brand costs less, it might be a better choice.

✓ **What is an ingredient?**

CRITICAL THINKING

Make Responsible Decisions

You want a snack. You can choose between two boxes of cereal. One is sugar coated. The other is not.

1. **Identify your choices. Check them out with your parent or trusted adult.** You could choose the sugary cereal or the other cereal.

2. **Evaluate each choice. Use the *Guidelines for Making Responsible Decisions™*.** Answer each question using both of your choices.

3. **Identify the responsible decision. Check this out with your parent or trusted adult.** Make your choice.

4. **Evaluate your decision.** Explain why your choice is responsible.

Guidelines for Making Responsible Decisions™

- Is it healthful?
- Is it safe?
- Does it follow rules and laws?
- Does it show respect for myself and others?
- Does it follow family guidelines?
- Does it show good character?

Planning a Menu

A food plan is also called a *menu*. You order from a menu at a restaurant. You may help your parents or guardian plan a family menu for one day.

How to Plan a Menu

You can plan a menu for healthful meals. Here's how.

- **Review the Dietary Guidelines.**
  The Dietary Guidelines are suggested goals for eating.

▶ When planning a menu, also include healthful snacks that may be eaten during the day. Foods from many countries around the world can be healthful snacks. Rice cakes are an example. So are tropical fruits such as papaya and bananas.

- **Follow MyPyramid.** Choose foods and drinks from each food group. This will help you get the right amounts from each food group. Include three meals and snacks in your menu.

- **Think about food safety.** Choose foods that do not need to be kept cold if you are going to a picnic.

You may choose healthful foods from many countries around the world. Eggplant dishes and chick peas are tasty examples. So are yucca and plantains. Tacos and pita sandwiches are favorite treats as well.

 What is a menu?

Health Online

Same Food, Different Price

Research and report on a food product that is sold at two different prices. Compare ingredients. Use the e-Journal writing tool to report your findings. Visit **www.mmhhealth.com** and click on ℮-Journal.

LESSON REVIEW

Review Concepts

1. **Name** three influences on your food choices.

2. **Explain** what kinds of information are found on food labels.

3. **Tell** how you can plan a menu for a healthful meal.

4. **Explain** why you might compare prices when shopping for a food item.

Critical Thinking

5. **Compare** The first three ingredients listed for one cereal are sugar, oats, and corn. The first three ingredients listed for another are oats, corn, and sugar. Which cereal has more sugar? How do you know?

6. **LIFE SKILLS** **Make Responsible Decisions** It's time for a snack. A friend offers to trade his candy bar for your apple. What should you do?

Analyze What Influences Your Health

Problem You are at a fast-food restaurant with a friend's family. Everything looks good. What influences your food choices?

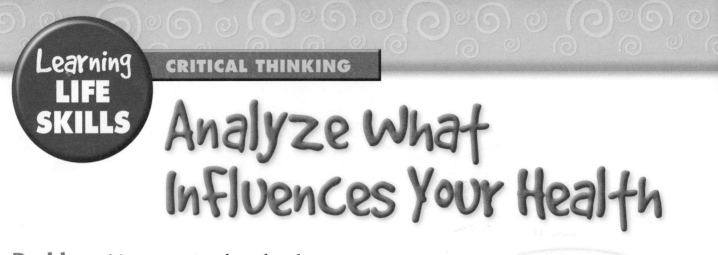

"The salad with chicken and cheese sounds healthy."

"I'm going to get that giant burger they show on TV."

"There are so many choices. I'm not sure what I want."

Solution You can analyze what influences your food choices. Use the four steps on the next page to help you.

Learn This Life Skill

Follow these four steps to help analyze what influences your food choices. The Foldables™ can help you.

1 **Identify people and things that can influence your health.**

Your friends influence your food choices. Who else might influence you?

2 **Evaluate how these people and things can affect your health.**

How do these influences affect your health? Record your ideas.

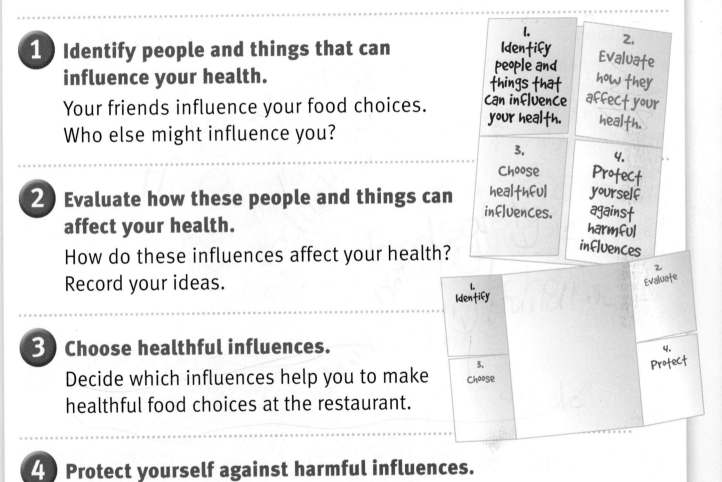

3 **Choose healthful influences.**

Decide which influences help you to make healthful food choices at the restaurant.

4 **Protect yourself against harmful influences.**

Be aware of influences that may result in unhealthful food choices at the restaurant.

Practice This Life Skill

Work with a group. Write a skit about what influences your food choices. Use the steps above.

Food Safety

You will learn . . .

- how food can be kept safe.

- how kitchen safety and table manners keep you safe.

Vocabulary

- **spoiled**, *B59*

You grab a jug of milk out of the refrigerator. Look at the date. This date can help tell you if the milk is still safe to drink. Reading dates is just one way to make sure food is safe to eat.

Keep Foods Safe

Foods and drinks can become **spoiled**. This means they are unsafe to eat. A food or drink spoils because germs grow on or in it. These germs can make you ill.

ACTIVITY

On Your Own
FOR SCHOOL OR HOME
Check Food Packages

Many foods and drinks have dates on their packages. These "use by" or expiration dates tell you when a food may not be safe to eat. Check the dates on foods and drinks in your refrigerator. Make a chart and keep track of all of the foods and their expiration dates. Decorate your chart and put it on your refrigerator.

Food Safety Tips

Prepare Food

- Wash your hands before you prepare food. Also wash them before you eat.
- Wash your hands after you touch raw meat or eggs.
- Wash fresh fruits and vegetables before you eat or cook them.
- Wash a cutting board that has been used to cut raw meat. Then you can use it to cut other foods.
- Check dates on foods and drinks before using them.

Cook Food

- Cooking kills germs. Cook meat well. A meat thermometer can be used to see if it has cooked enough.
- Do not eat foods with raw eggs. The eggs can contain germs. Unbaked cookie dough and cake batter may have raw eggs in them.

Clean Up

- Wrap leftovers quickly. Then put them into the refrigerator. Wrapping keeps germs off foods. Cold makes germs grow more slowly.
- Clean counters and cooking surfaces with soap and warm water. Dry with a paper towel.

 What makes food spoil?

Kitchen Safety and Table Manners

Do you like to help make meals? Do you enjoy eating with others? Stay safe. Follow kitchen safety rules when making meals. Use table manners when eating.

Kitchen Safety

When you work in the kitchen, be careful. Here are some safety rules.

- **Don't use a kitchen appliance unless your parent or guardian says it's okay.** A kitchen appliance (uh•PLY•uhns) is a small machine used for preparing food. Use it only with an adult.

- **Do not use an appliance near water or when you are wet.** You could get shocked.

- **Do not touch hot stove tops.** Hot stove tops cause burns.

- **Use pot holders.** This protects your hands from heat.

- **Never stick an object into a toaster.** You could get shocked.

- **Use a knife carefully.** Use it only with an adult.

- **Handle glasses and sharp utensils carefully.** You can cut yourself on broken glass or sharp blades.

▼ Be careful when you wash glasses and sharp utensils.

Use Table Manners

Table manners are polite ways to eat. Using table manners shows respect for others.

- Place your napkin in your lap to protect your clothing.
- Wait until everyone is served before you start eating.
- Chew with your mouth closed.
- Do not talk with your mouth full.

 Why is it important to use table manners?

ACTIVITY · LIFE SKILLS

CRITICAL THINKING

Practice Healthful Behaviors

You are going to a friend's house for dinner. How can you use table manners?

1. **Learn about a healthful behavior.** Identify the table manners you need to know before you go to dinner. Which will you use?

2. **Practice the behavior.** Practice the table manners when you visit your friend. Which table manners make eating safer and more pleasant?

3. **Ask for help if you need it.** If you have a question about table manners, ask.

4. **Make the behavior a habit.** Practice these manners at dinner. Write a paragraph about the manners you used.

LESSON REVIEW

Review Concepts

1. **Name** three ways to keep germs out of food.

2. **Describe** how to clean counters and cooking surfaces after you have prepared food.

3. **Explain** why you should not talk with your mouth full.

Critical Thinking

4. **Infer** Why should you use a kitchen appliance only when a parent or guardian is watching?

5. **LIFE SKILLS** **Practice Healthful Behaviors** Suppose you are helping to wash dishes. Why should you check carefully before you reach into the dishwater?

CHAPTER 4 REVIEW

Use Vocabulary

diet, *B39*

Dietary Guidelines, *B45*

MyPyramid, *B40*

food label, *B52*

nutrients, *B39*

spoiled, *B59*

vitamins, *B39*

Choose the correct term from the list to complete each sentence.

1. The guide that tells you the amounts from each food group your body needs every day is __?__.

2. The materials in food that are used by the body are __?__.

3. The food and drink usually eaten by a person is called a(n) __?__.

4. The __?__ are suggested goals to help you stay healthy and live longer.

5. When foods and drinks become __?__, they are unsafe to eat.

6. Nutrients that help your body use other nutrients are called __?__.

7. A(n) __?__ lists the ingredients and nutrition facts of a packaged food item.

Review Concepts

Answer each question in complete sentences.

8. What nutrient is the body's main energy source?

9. How can you use MyPyramid to plan a healthful diet?

10. What are three influences on your food choices?

11. Why is it unsafe to eat uncooked cookie dough?

12. What are table manners?

Reading Comprehension

Answer each question in complete sentences.

The Vegetable Group is the green food group in MyPyramid. You need to eat 2 1/2 cups from this group daily. Foods in the Vegetable Group give you vitamins, minerals, and carbohydrates.

13. What is the green food group in MyPyramid?

14. How many cups of vegetables should you eat each day?

15. Why is it healthful to eat different vegetables for each meal?

Critical Thinking/Problem Solving

Answer each question in complete sentences.

Analyze Concepts

16. What can you learn from reading a food label?

17. Explain why you should eat some whole grain foods each day.

18. Give three reasons you should not drink alcohol.

19. List the kinds of nutrients the body needs. Why is each nutrient important?

20. Why is it important to wrap and refrigerate leftover foods promptly?

Practice Life Skills

21. **Analyze What Influences Your Health** Some snacks that are sold in stores do not follow Dietary Guidelines. What influences may make you want to buy healthful snacks?

22. **Make Responsible Decisions** You are spending the night at a friend's house. Your friend offers you a fruit drink. Your parent or guardian does not want you to drink fruit drinks because they are high in sugar. What should you do? Use the *Guidelines for Making Responsible Decisions*™ to help you decide.

Read Graphics

The chart shows the amounts from each food group a person should eat daily. How much did John eat? Use the chart to answer questions 23–24.

Food Group	Recommended Amount	Number of servings John ate in one day
Meat and Beans	5 oz.	6 oz.
Milk	3 cups	3 cups
Fruits	1 1/2 cups	1 1/2 cups
Vegetables	2 1/2 cups	1/2 cup
Grains	6 oz.	6 oz.

23. From which food groups did John get the recommended amount of food?

24. From which food group did John have an extra amount?

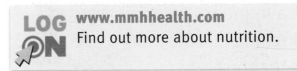
LOG ON www.mmhhealth.com
Find out more about nutrition.

Effective Communication

Make a Poster

Make a poster that lists safety rules for preparing food. Draw pictures to go with the list. Hang the poster in your kitchen.

Self-Directed Learning

Make a Timeline

Visit the library or interview an adult. Learn about the changes that happen to people as they grow from birth to your age. When do they learn to walk? When do they start losing baby teeth? Make a timeline showing when changes happen.

Critical Thinking and Problem Solving

Plan a Menu

Some people don't eat meat. They are vegetarians. Plan a healthful menu that doesn't have meat. Include breakfast, lunch, and dinner.

Responsible Citizenship

Donate Food

Some families do not have the healthful foods they need. Ask your parent or guardian if you can donate food to a food pantry to help these families. Choose foods and drinks that are healthful.

Personal Health and Safety

CHAPTER 5

Personal Health and Physical Activity

What Do You Know?

Do you practice healthful habits? Answer **yes** or **no** to the following health habits.

__?__ I floss and brush my teeth every day.

__?__ I use proper lighting to protect my eyes when I read or watch television.

__?__ I wash my hair with shampoo.

__?__ I stretch before I exercise.

__?__ I wear a helmet when I ride my bike.

Did you answer **yes** to all five statements? If so, you are practicing healthful habits. Read **Personal Health and Physical Activity** to learn about these and other health habits.

LOG ON www.mmhhealth.com
Find out more about personal health and physical activity.

C3

Checkups and Dental Health

You will learn . . .

- why you need medical checkups.
- why you need to keep your teeth healthy.
- how to floss and brush your teeth.

Vocabulary

- **checkup**, *C5*
- **dental plaque**, *C6*
- **cavity**, *C6*
- **dental floss**, *C7*

You can take action to stay healthy. You can wash your face everyday. You can get the proper amount of sleep each night. Having regular checkups can help you stay healthy, too.

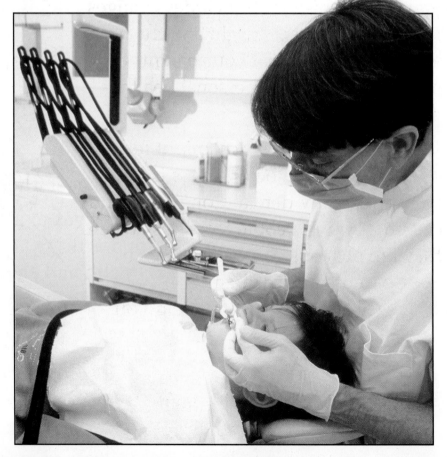

Medical Checkups

A doctor's job has many parts. Doctors help people who are ill. Sometimes they give ill people medicine. They might give advice, too.

Doctors also help people stay well. They give checkups. A **checkup** is a medical exam to make sure you are healthy. During a checkup, the doctor measures your height and weight. The doctor checks your eyes, ears, nose, and throat. He or she checks your lungs and heart. Checkups help you and your doctor notice changes in your health.

Personal Health Record Your doctor keeps a health record on you. A personal health record tells facts about your health history. It includes changes in your weight and height and the times you were ill. You and your parents or guardian can keep a personal health record at home.

Going to the Doctor You might feel stress seeing the doctor. *Stress* is the response to any demand on your mind or body. Young people feel stress when they are nervous or excited. Talk to your parents or guardian about your feelings. Talking may help you feel better.

 Why is it important to have regular medical checkups?

CAREERS
Pediatrician

A pediatrician is a doctor who takes care of babies and children. Their growth and development is very important. A pediatrician looks for changes in a child's health. He or she can help a child make a health plan.

LOG ON www.mmhhealth.com Find out more about health careers.

▲ **A doctor who takes care of children is called a pediatrician.**

C5

Healthy Teeth

There are three ways healthy teeth help you. They give you a nice smile. They help you speak clearly. They bite and chew food. As you chew pieces of food can stick to your teeth. This food mixes with germs in your mouth. Then a sticky material called **dental plaque** forms on your teeth. If dental plaque stays on your teeth, a cavity may form. A **cavity** is a hole in a tooth.

A dental health plan can help keep your teeth and gums healthy.

Parts of a Tooth

- **Crown** The part above the gums

- **Enamel** A hard, white material that covers the crown

- **Dentin** Bony layer under the enamel

- **Pulp** The soft, inner part that has nerves and blood vessels

- **Root** Holds the tooth in the jawbone

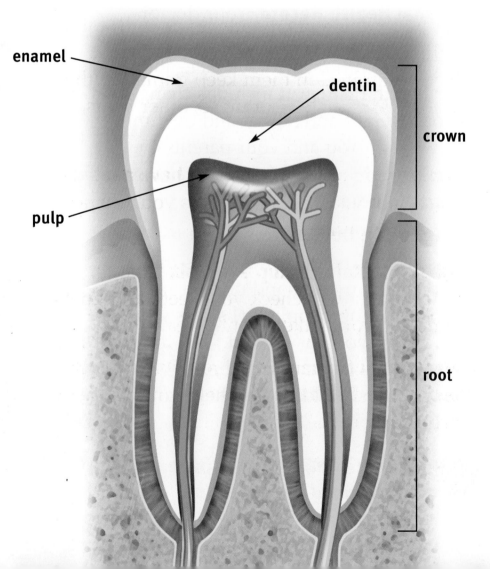

enamel

dentin

crown

pulp

root

Your Hair

Wash your hair with shampoo to remove dirt and oil. Use shampoo that is made for your hair type. Conditioner coats hair and makes it easier to comb.

Sharing hats, brushes, or combs with others can spread head lice. Head lice, shown on page C16, are tiny insects that lay eggs in the hair. To treat head lice, use a special shampoo that kills the lice and eggs.

Your Nails

Your nails protect the ends of your fingers and toes. Trimming your nails is part of good grooming. Nails that are trimmed and smooth are less likely to be damaged. Clean nails by washing them with soap and water. Do not bite your nails or pick at the skin around the nails.

 What is an important part of grooming skin, hair, and nails?

Do You Know?

The longer the finger, the faster the nail grows. The nail on the middle finger grows the fastest. Fingernails also grow faster than toenails. Toenails are thicker than fingernails.

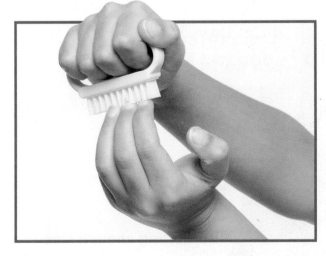

▲ **Use a nail brush to clean under nails.**

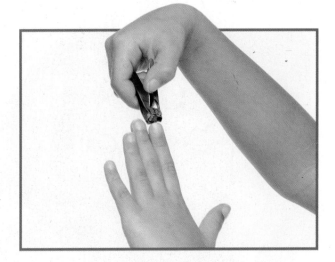

▲ **Trim your nails regularly. Clip them straight across. File rough edges.**

Rest and Sleep

ACTIVITY

Math
L I N K

Sleep Graph

Keep track of the hours you sleep each night for a week. Make a bar graph of your findings. How many nights did you get ten to twelve hours of sleep?

People your age need ten to twelve hours of sleep each night. Getting enough rest and sleep helps you stay alert in school. It keeps you from being tired and having accidents or getting ill. Here are ways to get plenty of sleep at night.

- **Get plenty of physical activity.** Try to be physically active every day. Walk, bike, or skate.

- **Relax before going to bed.** Read a book, look at a magazine, listen to soft music, or talk with family members.

- **Do not eat or drink caffeine.** Caffeine will keep you awake.

- **Do not go to bed angry or upset.** Talk about your feelings if you are upset or angry.

- **Keep a regular schedule.** Go to bed at the same time each night. Get up at the same time each morning.

✓ **Name three things you can do to get plenty of sleep at night.**

◄ **Getting enough sleep will help you do well in school.**

Be a Health Advocate

Work in a small group. Write a skit about healthy sleep tips. Perform the skit for the class.

1 **Choose a healthful action to communicate.**
As a group, choose an action that will help you get the proper rest.

2 **Collect information about the action.**
Determine why this action helps people get proper rest. Use your textbook or school library to find information.

3 **Decide how to communicate this information.**
Will the skit show a healthful action? Decide what the skit will show.

4 **Communicate your message to others.**
Perform the skit in front of the class. Other groups should decide whether the action performed is healthful or not.

LESSON REVIEW

Review Concepts

1. **Define** the word grooming.

2. **Discuss** how to care for your hair and nails.

3. **Explain** ways to get a good night's sleep.

Critical Thinking

4. **Infer** Monday night you use a new shampoo. Tuesday morning your scalp itches. What could be a reason that your scalp itches?

5. **LIFE SKILLS** **Be a Health Advocate**
Design a poster. Show how to prevent the spread of lice. What information will you include?

Physical Activity

You will learn . . .

- why being physically active is important.
- how you can work on physical fitness.

Vocabulary

- **physical fitness,** *C21*
- **heart fitness,** *C22*
- **low body fat,** *C22*
- **muscle endurance,** *C22*
- **muscle strength,** *C22*
- **flexibility,** *C22*

Running, biking, and playing tennis are all physical activities. It is important to get plenty of physical activity. When you are physically active, you become physically fit. When you are physically fit, you have energy to work and play.

Benefits of Physical Fitness

Physical fitness means having your body in good shape. Your heart, lungs, bones, joints, and muscles stay strong when you are fit. You can move with ease when you are fit. People become physically fit through regular activity.

Keeping physically fit cuts the risk of disease. It helps you keep a healthful weight. Regular activity improves blood flow to the brain, keeping your mind clear and sharp. You might do better in school, too.

One type of physical activity is swimming. Swimming is an aerobic exercise. Aerobic exercises help condition the heart and lungs.

 How does being physically active improve your mind?

Physical Health Physical activity helps keep your heart, lungs, bones, joints, and muscles strong. It helps you stay at a healthful weight.

Mental and Emotional Health Physical activity can help you manage stress. Being physically fit helps you have a healthful self-concept.

Family and Social Health Making friends that care about physical fitness helps your family and social health. You and your friends can be active together. Your family can be active together.

Kinds of Health Fitness

The five kinds of fitness are listed below.

- **Heart fitness** is the condition of your heart and blood vessels. A strong heart pushes more blood out each time it beats. Between beats, a strong heart has longer to rest. Biking and running improve heart fitness.

- **Low body fat** is having a lean body without too much fat. Body fat is tested with skinfold calipers (KA•luh•puhrs). These are used to squeeze fat on your arm. The thickness tells how much body fat you have. Swimming and running help lower body fat.

- **Muscle endurance** is the ability to use your muscles for a long time. Swimming laps, walking, and running can improve muscle endurance.

- **Muscle strength** is the ability of your muscles to lift, pull, kick, and throw. Sit-ups and pull-ups help make your muscles strong.

- **Flexibility** is the ability to bend and move easily. Stretching your muscles helps them become more flexible. Gymnastics and dancing are two activities that require flexibility.

Your Physical Fitness Plan

You can make a physical fitness plan to keep track of your physical activity. A **physical fitness plan** is a written plan of physical activities. You can use the plan to help you stay fit. You can keep track of the activities you do each week.

Steps to make your physical fitness plan:

1. Make a calendar for one week.
2. Make time on three to five days to work on heart fitness and low body fat.
3. Make time on two to four days to work on muscle strength and endurance.
4. Make time on two to three days to work on flexibility.

 How many days should you work on muscle strength and endurance?

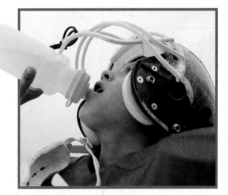

▲ **Drink lots of water and sports drinks when it is hot outside so that you don't get dehydrated.**

▼ **Here is a sample physical fitness plan.**

Physical Fitness Plan

Sunday	Monday	Tuesday	Wednesday	Thursday	Friday	Saturday
Muscle strength: Do 15 pull-ups	Heart Fitness: Ride bike for 30 minutes	Flexibility: Practice gymnastics for 20 minutes	Heart Fitness: Jog for 30 minutes	Muscle strength: Do 30 sit-ups	Heart Fitness: Ride bike for 30 minutes	Flexibility: Dance for 30 minutes
Muscle Endurance: Walk for 30 minutes	Low Body Fat: Jog for 20 minutes		Low Body Fat: Ride bike for 20 minutes	Muscle Endurance: Swim 10 laps	Low Body Fat: Jog for 20 minutes	

Warm-Up and Cool-Down

Every workout should include a warm-up and a cool-down. A **warm-up** is three to five minutes of easy physical activity done before a workout. This could include knee lifts, arm circles, walking, or slow jogging. A warm-up helps prevent muscle injuries. It prepares your muscles for physical activity. A **cool-down** is five to ten minutes of easy physical activity done after a workout. Walking and stretching might be part of a cool-down. A cool-down helps your muscles relax after a workout.

 Why is it important to warm-up before you begin physical activity?

▶ After you run, you should do cool-down exercises to relax your muscles.

C28

Practice Healthful Behaviors

Work with a partner. Write a television commercial about jogging. State that jogging is a healthful behavior.

1 **Learn about a healthful behavior.** Use your textbook or school library to learn about jogging. Find out how jogging improves a person's health.

2 **Practice the behavior.** In the commercial tell how jogging helps to improve health. Suggest places to jog.

3 **Ask for help if you need it.** Show your commercial to your physical education teacher. Have him or her give you advice on how to make your commercial better.

4 **Make the behavior a habit.** Present your television commercial to the class. Discuss how each student can make jogging a habit.

LESSON REVIEW

Review Concepts

1. **Describe** a physical fitness plan.

2. **List** three physical activities that you can do at home with your family to stay in shape.

3. **Identify** physical activities that you can you do to improve agility.

Critical Thinking

4. **Analyze** how warming up and cooling down prevent injury.

5. **LIFE SKILLS** **Practice Healthful Behaviors** Name a healthful behavior you can practice before a workout to prevent injury.

Safety and Physical Activity

You will learn . . .

- ways to prevent injuries during physical activity.
- what safety equipment is needed for different sports.
- ways to be a good sport.

Vocabulary

- **safety equipment**, *C32*
- **mouthguard**, *C32*

Games and sports are more fun if you stay safe while playing them! That's why safety equipment is needed for some sports. There are other ways to prevent you and others from being injured, too.

Ways to Prevent Injuries

There are ways to prevent injuries during physical activities.

Follow the Rules Rules help keep you and others from injury. Respect other players in every activity. Do not hit or push other players. Following rules helps you build healthful relationships.

When to Stop Stop playing if you are tired or have an injury. Tell your coach, parents or guardian. If you keep playing, you could make an injury worse.

Choose a Safe Place to Play Do not play where there may be broken glass or holes. Do not play where there may be moving cars or trucks, or people who might try to harm you. Tell your parents or guardian where you will be playing. A coach or another adult should watch you play sports.

▲ Safe equipment helps keep children safe while they play.

 Why should you follow the rules of the game or sport you are playing?

Safety Equipment

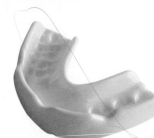

▲ Up to one-third of all dental injuries happen during sports. Wear a mouthguard during sports in which you might fall or be hit in the mouth by a person, ball, or puck.

Safety equipment protects you from injuries when you play sports or exercise. Do you wear a helmet when you ride your bike? A bike helmet is a type of safety equipment.

Special clothing keeps skin from being scraped, cut, or bruised. Knee pads, elbow pads, and wrist pads protect bones and joints from injury. Safety glasses protect the eyes. In some sports, boys need to wear a protective cup.

A **mouthguard** is an object worn to protect the mouth and teeth. Some sports require all athletes to wear a mouthguard.

▲ **Football** Wear a helmet, pads, and mouthguard to protect your head, body, and mouth.

▲ **Ice Hockey** Wear a helmet, padded guards, gloves and a face mask.

▲ **Soccer** Wear shin guards.

To protect you from injury, safety equipment has to fit. Gear that is too small is uncomfortable. You may not be able to move easily. Gear that is too large may move or come off. Gear should be worn the proper way, with all straps tightened, fastened, and secure.

 What can happen if your safety gear does not fit properly?

▲ **Baseball** Wear a helmet when at bat. Catchers wear a helmet, face mask, knee and chest guards, and a protective cup.

▲ **Biking** Wear a helmet and shoes with closed toes. Ride a bike with reflectors on the frame, wheels, and pedals.

▲ **Inline Skating** Wear a helmet, elbow and knee pads, and wrist guards.

Be a Good Sport

▲ Shaking hands with members of the other team is one way to be a good sport.

You need more than fitness skills to play sports. You need to get along with your teammates. You need to cooperate with them. To *cooperate* is to work well with others toward a goal. This is one way to be a good sport.

There are other ways to be a good sport. Show respect for your teammates. Respect players on other teams, too. Never hit, shove, or kick other players. Do not use wrong language or tease other players. Follow the rules of the game. Listen to the coach or team leader.

▲ Be a good sport when you are a fan, too.

If you lose, you may feel disappointed. But don't feel sad or blame others for losing. Work harder to do better next time. Everyone will enjoy the game if you all have fun as you play.

Wait your turn when you are sharing at a playground. Follow rules on the safety signs. Sometimes there are rules for how to use a diving board or bike path. These rules help keep you and others safe.

 List two ways that you can be a good sport when you play with others.

ACTIVITY

LIFE SKILLS — CRITICAL THINKING

Resolve Conflicts

Role-play a conflict between Timmy and Jamal. Each role-player will have a partner who will help resolve conflict.

1. **Stay calm.** Timmy pushes Jamal as he goes for a lay up. Jamal's partner tells him how to respond.

2. **Talk about the conflict.** Jamal does what his partner says.

3. **List possible ways to settle the conflict.** Jamal and Timmy's partners' tell them what to say or do.

4. **Agree on a way to settle the conflict. You may need to ask a responsible adult for help.** Jamal and Timmy do what their partners say. The class decides if Jamal and Timmy chose the best way to resolve the conflict.

LESSON REVIEW

Review Concepts

1. **Explain** why it is important to choose a safe place to play sports and games.

2. **List** three examples of safety equipment.

3. **Explain** ways you can be a good sport.

Critical Thinking

4. **Summarize** ways different kinds of safety equipment helps protect you from injury.

5. **LIFE SKILLS** **Resolve Conflicts** Half the students in your class want to play basketball, while the other half want to play volleyball. Both games cannot be played on one court at the same time. List possible ways to settle the conflict.

Use Communication Skills

Problem Sam, Justin, and Desmond want to play a game. They are all talking at the same time.

Solution It is important to be able to communicate well while playing games. The friends decide to use communication skills.

Learn This Life Skill

These steps will help the friends communicate. The Foldables™ can help.

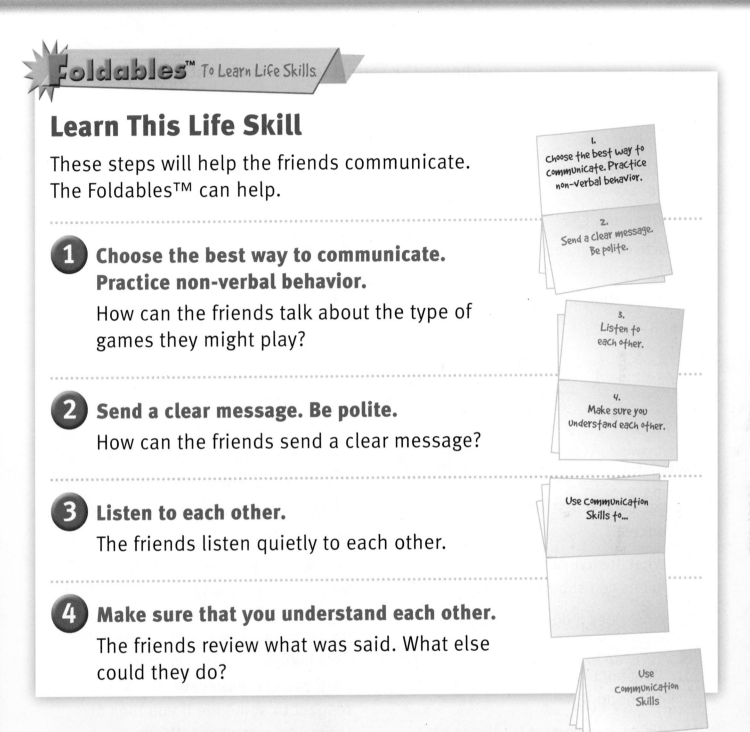

1 **Choose the best way to communicate. Practice non-verbal behavior.**

How can the friends talk about the type of games they might play?

2 **Send a clear message. Be polite.**

How can the friends send a clear message?

3 **Listen to each other.**

The friends listen quietly to each other.

4 **Make sure that you understand each other.**

The friends review what was said. What else could they do?

Practice This Life Skill

Work in groups of six. Have everyone speak at the same time. What happened? Now try taking turns. How did communication improve?

Use Vocabulary

dental plaque, *C6*

flexibility, *C22*

grooming, *C16*

health-care product, *C16*

mouthguard, *C32*

muscle endurance, *C22*

physical fitness, *C21*

warm–up, *C28*

Choose the correct term from the list to complete each sentence.

1. You should always ___?___ at the beginning of a workout.

2. Taking care of your body and appearance is called ___?___.

3. Having your body in top condition is called ___?___.

4. You can protect your mouth and teeth from injury during physical activity by wearing a ___?___.

5. A product used for grooming is called a(n) ___?___.

6. The ability to use your muscles for a long time is called ___?___.

7. The ability to bend and move easily is called ___?___.

8. A sticky material that forms on teeth is called ___?___.

Review Concepts

Answer each question in complete sentences.

9. What are five healthful grooming habits you should practice?

10. What does a doctor do during a medical checkup?

11. What should you do if your eyes itch or burn?

12. Why is it important to choose physical activities you enjoy doing for your physical fitness plan?

13. What are three sports that can help you improve agility?

Reading Comprehension

Answer each question in complete sentences.

You rely on your sense of sight, or **vision**, in many ways. Your eyes help you stay safe. For example, you look up and down the street to check for cars before crossing. Your eyes also help you communicate. You show respect to someone if you look at them while you are talking.

14. What does *vision* mean?

15. What is one way that your eyes help you stay safe?

16. How do your eyes help you communicate with others?

Critical Thinking/Problem Solving

Answer each question in complete sentences.

Analyze Concepts

17. After you get to the hockey rink, you realize you forgot your safety equipment. Explain how not wearing safety gear might cause injury.

18. At football practice, you find that your helmet is too big. Explain why it is important for your safety gear to fit properly.

19. You are accidentally hit with a pitch. Tell why it is important to be a good sport at such times.

20. Explain how lack of sleep affects your health. Name two ways you can get plenty of sleep each night.

Practice Life Skills

21. **Use Communication Skills** Your older sister is playing loud music. You cannot do your homework. How can you use communication skills to solve this problem?

22. **Make Responsible Decisions** You don't have your safety equipment with you, but your friends want you to play soccer anyway. What should you do?

Read Graphics

The chart lists the decibels of five sounds. Decibels measure how loud or soft a sound is. Use it to answer questions 23–25.

Sound	Decibels
Whisper	30
Talking in a normal voice	60
Lawnmower	90
Chainsaw	100
Jet plane engine	140

23. Sounds louder than 85 decibels can cause hearing loss. Which of the sounds on the chart could cause hearing loss?

24. Calculate how much higher in decibels a chainsaw is than your normal talking voice.

25. Decide if the decibels of a lawnmower are lower or higher than the decibels of a jet plane engine.

 LOG ON www.mmhhealth.com Find out how much you know about personal health and physical activity.

CHAPTER 6

Violence and Injury Prevention

What Do You Know?

You can stay safe and have fun at the same time. Look at the list of safety equipment below. Which equipment do you wear when you bike, skate, or ride a scooter?

- __?__ helmet
- __?__ wrist pads
- __?__ elbow pads
- __?__ knee pads

Did you check all of the equipment? If so, you have been practicing safety rules. Read **Violence and Injury Prevention** to learn more about safety.

LOG ON www.mmhhealth.com
Find out more about preventing violence and injury.

STOP

CHOOL KING

Indoor Safety

You will learn . . .

- how to prevent falls.
- how to prevent fires.
- ways to avoid injury from poisons.
- what computer safety means.

Suppose you leave your toys in the middle of the floor. Someone could trip over them and get hurt. Remember to put your toys away to prevent injuries. This is an important safety rule. Following safety rules can help keep you safe.

Vocabulary

- **accident**, *C43*
- **injury**, *C43*
- **hazard**, *C43*
- **fire escape plan**, *C45*
- **poison**, *C47*

Follow Safety Rules

An **accident** is something that is not supposed to happen. An **injury** is damage or harm done to a person. Most injuries are caused by accidents.

Suppose someone leaves a skate on the floor. You trip on the skate. The skate is a safety hazard. A **hazard** is something that can cause harm or injury. The following safety rules can help you prevent accidents.

How to Prevent Accidents

At Home You can take steps to help your parents or guardian make home a safe place.

- **Put away toys, books, and other objects.** These items are tripping hazards.

- **Use a stepstool to reach things up high.** First get permission from an adult.

- **Try not to walk on wet floors.** Wet floors are slippery and dangerous.

At School You can follow safety rules in school, too.

- **Keep the floor free of objects.** That way you won't make a tripping hazard.

- **Walk in the hallways.** Watch for other people so that you don't bump into them.

▲ **Try not to walk on wet floors.**

 Why is it important to follow safety rules?

▲ STOP! Do not run. That can make things worse.

▲ DROP to the ground.

▲ ROLL back and forth to put out the flames. Cover your face with your hands.

Safety Rules to Prevent Fire

You can help keep your home safe from fire.

- **Have your parents check smoke alarm batteries.** Smoke alarm batteries should be checked at least twice a year.

- **Call for help if you see a fire.** Dial 9-1-1.

- **Practice Stop, Drop, and Roll.** If your clothes catch on fire, you should stop, drop, and roll. This will put the fire out.

Electricity: Play it Safe

Use an electric appliance only if your parent or guardian is there to help you.

Electrical cords and extension cords should be used safely. Don't use appliances if their cords are damaged. Don't put them under carpets or across doorways.

Don't plug more appliances into an outlet than it can hold. The outlet could heat up and catch fire.

In Case of Fire

You and your family should have a fire escape plan. A **fire escape plan** is a map of your home that shows different ways out of every room. Your plan should include two ways out of each room and a place to meet your family outside.

 What should you do if you are trapped inside a room during a fire?

▲ The first way out of a fire should be a door. Feel a door before you open it. If it is hot, don't open it. If the door is cool, open it a crack. Check for smoke.

▼ If it is smoky, crawl on your hands and knees to keep below the line of smoke. Cover your mouth and nose. If you can't do these things, close the door and cover the bottom with a towel. Go to a window and yell for help.

What Is Computer Safety?

People use computers to write reports and do research on the Internet. The Internet has sites that are not safe for children. Also, strangers may be able to find out private information about you on the Internet. Play it safe when using the Internet. Here are some tips for you.

- **Use the Internet** only when your parent or guardian gives you permission.

- **Do not give out** your name, address, telephone number, age, photo, school, parents' names, or other personal information.

- **Tell your parent or guardian** if anyone tries to find out where you live or tries to meet you.

Why is it important not to give out personal information on the Internet?

◀ Only use the Internet when your parent or guardian is with you.

ACTIVITY

On Your Own

FOR SCHOOL OR HOME

Surfer Safety Reminder

RULE: For safety's sake, never surf the Internet alone. To remember this rule, make a surfer T-shirt. Ask your parents or guardian to buy you a plain white T-shirt. With a permanent marker, write across the front of the T-shirt: *Surf With A Parent Only.* Decorate your T-shirt with permanent markers of different colors.

Poison Control

A **poison** is a drug or substance that harms or kills. Eating or drinking poison, or breathing in its fumes, is harmful. A poison can also cause harm by entering a person's body through the skin.

A parent or guardian should always help you use household products. Move away and get fresh air if you smell a strong odor. Keep household products in their own labeled containers and away from young children.

 How can someone be harmed by a poison?

Practice Healthful Behaviors

1. **Learn about a healthful behavior.** Learn how to make a fire escape plan for your home.

2. **Practice the behavior.** Practice your plan with your family. Use the door as the exit when you practice.

3. **Ask for help if you need it.** Have your parents or guardian review your plan. Agree on a place to meet outside.

4. **Make the behavior a habit.** Have home fire drills every month.

Bathroom · Mom and Dad's Room · Kitchen · Living Room · My room

▶ Every family should have a fire escape plan.

LESSON REVIEW

Review Concepts

1. **Describe** three ways you can prevent falls at home.

2. **Explain** how you can prevent injuries caused by electricity.

3. **Discuss** why you should use the Internet safely.

4. **Name** two ways to protect yourself around poisons.

Critical Thinking

5. **Comprehend** A young child visits your home. The cleaning materials are kept in a low cabinet. How could the child be harmed? How could you help prevent it?

6. **LIFE SKILLS** **Practice Healthful Behaviors** You see that your family does not have a fire escape plan. What healthful behavior can you work on to keep safe in case of a fire?

Safety on the Go

You will learn . . .

- how to keep safe around cars and buses.
- safety rules when walking, biking, skating, and riding a scooter.
- how to keep safe around water.

Vocabulary

- **seat belt**, *C49*
- **personal flotation device**, *C52*

A common way to travel is by car. Another way is by bus. Do you ride a bus to school? Do your parents or guardian drop you off in a car? There are safety rules for each of these ways to travel.

Safety on the Go

People use buses and cars to travel from one place to another. Some people take a bus to work. Others use a car. You might ride on a bus to go on a school field trip. Maybe you ride in a car with your family to the grocery store. You should follow safety rules when you ride in buses and cars.

Always wear a seat belt when you ride in a car. A **seat belt** is the lap and shoulder belt worn in a car. Ride in the back seat. It is safer than riding in the front seat. Lock the door when you are seated. Get out on the curb side of the car.

Follow these safety rules when taking a bus.

- **When waiting for a bus** try to take at least four giant steps away from the curb.

- **Never walk behind a bus.** The bus driver can't see you.

- **Cross only in front of the bus.** Wait for the driver to signal that it is okay to cross the street.

- **On the bus, sit quietly in your seat.** Keep aisles clear.

 What can you do to keep safe while riding on a bus?

▲ **Find the Right Seat Belt.** Each seat in a car has its own belt. Make sure that you have the right belt for your seat.

▲ **Pull the Belt Across Your Lap.** Sit up straight. Pull the belt from your shoulder down to the opposite hip.

▲ **Snap the Belt Tight Around Your Hips.** Snap the two sections of the belt together. Make sure that the belt is tight around your hips.

Safety and Sports Vehicles

When you walk, skate, bike, or ride a scooter, you should follow safety rules to stay safe.

Skating and Riding Scooters

Wear a helmet, elbow pads, wrist guards, and knee pads when you skate or ride a scooter. Do not skate or ride in traffic. Skate or ride on smooth areas. Do not skate or ride at night. Use hand signals so that other people will know what you are going to do.

Right Turn
Stretch out your left arm, bend at the elbow, and point your forearm up.

Left Turn
Stretch out your left arm, with your forearm extended out.

Stop
Use your left arm. Bend your elbow down. Your palm faces the back to show stop signal.

Riding a Bike

You might ride a bike to school. Or, you might ride your bike with your friends for fun. Follow these rules to stay safe.

- **Always wear a helmet flat on the top of your head.** Make sure that the helmet fits you.

- **Ride your bike on a bicycle path when possible.** If you ride on a street or road, ride on the right hand side.

- **Ride only in daylight.** People cannot see you at night.

- **Stop and look both ways when you cross a street with your bike.** Walk your bike across the street.

- **Don't wear long pants that are loose at the ankle.** They could get caught in the bike and cause you to crash.

 Describe a safe area to skate.

ACTIVITY

On Your Own

FOR SCHOOL OR HOME

Make a Poster

Make a poster showing safety rules for riding a bike. Ask for permission to display your poster at home.

▼ **Always follow safety rules when you ride bicycles and skate.**

Water Sports

Playing in or near water can be fun. Follow these safety rules when you swim and boat.

Swimming

Follow these safety rules when you swim.

- **Learn to swim.** Take swimming lessons. A swimming teacher can show you how to swim.
- **Wear sunscreen when you swim outside.** Sunscreen will protect your skin from the Sun.
- **Swim with a lifeguard on duty.** Do not swim by yourself. Swim with a parent, guardian or trusted adult.
- **Swim only where signs say that swimming is allowed.** It is not safe to swim in every area.
- **Do not go in deep water.** Do not go in water that is above your head.

Riding in a Boat

Follow these rules when you ride in a boat.

- **Always wear a personal flotation device** (PFD), an object that helps you stay afloat in water.
- **Do not hang over the side of the boat.** You could fall out.
- **Stay seated.** It is easy to tip a small boat if you stand up in it.

▲ Always wear a personal flotation device when you are on a boat. What other safe practices do you see here?

How can you swim safely?

Make Responsible Decisions

Aza wants to swim in a lake with no one watching. Help Aza make a responsible decision.

1 **Identify your choices. Check them out with your parent or trusted adult.** Write three choices Aza could make on a three-column chart.

2 **Evaluate each choice. Use the *Guidelines for Making Responsible Decisions™*.** Write your responses on the chart.

3 **Identify the responsible decision. Check this out with your parent or trusted adult.** Write the decision at the bottom of the chart.

4 **Evaluate your decision.** Discuss possible outcomes of the decision.

Guidelines for Making Responsible Decisions™

- **Is it healthful?**
- **Is it safe?**
- **Does it follow rules and laws?**
- **Does it show respect for myself and others?**
- **Does it follow my family's guidelines?**
- **Does it show good character?**

LESSON REVIEW

Review Concepts

1. **List** three safety rules for riding in a car.

2. **Explain** how to cross the street safely after leaving a school bus.

3. **Compare** the safety rules for riding a bike and for skating.

4. **Name** three safety rules to follow while riding in a boat.

Critical Thinking

5. **Analyze** A friend wants to swim far out from the beach to see how deep the water is. Is your friend following safety rules? Explain.

6. **LIFE SKILLS** **Make Responsible Decisions** You see a friend across the street. You want to cross. You are halfway down the street. What is the responsible decision? How could you use the decision making steps to decide?

Safe in Wind and Weather

You will learn . . .

- how to stay safe outdoors.
- how to stay safe in bad weather.

Vocabulary

- **thunderstorm**, *C56*
- **flood**, *C56*
- **earthquake**, *C56*
- **tornado**, *C57*

What activities do you enjoy outdoors? Do you visit the playground? Perhaps you enjoy swinging on the monkey bars. What should you do if the weather suddenly turns bad? You should go inside right away.

Outdoor Safety

When you run and play outdoors, it is important to be safe. Make sure to follow these safety rules. These rules will help keep you safe on or near playgrounds.

- Don't play on equipment that is broken.
- Don't tie ropes to equipment. You could get tangled.
- Don't try stunts or dares.
- Make sure that a responsible adult is nearby.

More Outdoor Safety Rules

- Check that your shoelaces are tied when you run.
- Don't climb trees, telephone poles or power poles.
- Don't run near a swimming pool or on wet ground. You could slip and fall.

 Why should you not tie ropes to playground equipment?

▶ **Keep your shoes tied so that you don't trip.**

ACTIVITY

Physical Education

L I N K

Hurling Safety Rules

Play with the whole class or with a partner. You will need a beach ball. Stand in a large circle (or facing a partner). Begin by tossing the ball to a player. As the player catches the ball, he or she names an outdoor safety rule. Then he or she tosses the ball to another player. Keep going until all the rules have been named.

Natural Disasters

Natural disasters are events caused by nature. They result in heavy damage. Storms, floods, and earthquakes are natural disasters. You can stay safe in them.

Thunderstorm

A **thunderstorm** is a storm with thunder and lightning. Follow these safety rules to stay safe.

- **Go inside.** You will be safer from lightning when indoors.
- **Do not use the telephone.** Lightning can travel through wires.
- **Keep away from water.** Lightning can travel through some plumbing pipes.

Flood

A **flood** is the overflow of water onto dry land. Do not go into flood water. Listen to the radio for emergency information.

Earthquake

An **earthquake** is a shaking or trembling of the ground. To protect yourself, drop to the floor and get under something for cover, such as a desk, or stand in a doorway. Stay away from glass, windows, and bookcases. Move away from buildings and electrical wires if you are outdoors.

Do You Know?

Thunderstorm Fact

Lightning strikes before rain falls. Safety Tip: Stop activities and take shelter when you see lightning. Do not wait for rain.

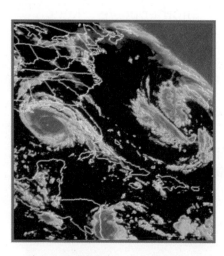

▲ **Satellites are used to track harmful weather conditions. This kind of technolgy can help save lives.**

Follow Safety Rules for a Tornado

A **tornado** is a powerful storm with winds that whirl in a dark cloud. Follow these safety rules to keep yourself safe during a tornado.

- **Go indoors.** If you can't get indoors, lie in a low area.

- **Go to a basement** or go to the center of a ground floor.

- **Stay away from windows.** The glass could blow out of the window and cut you.

 How can you stay safe during a tornado?

Access Health Facts, Products, and Services

1 **Identify when you might need health facts, products, and services.** Suppose a bad storm is coming toward your town. You need to know how to protect yourself.

2 **Identify where you might find health facts, products, and services.** Find information about storms using your textbook.

3 **Find the health facts, products, and services you need.** Identify two sources of information about storms.

4 **Evaluate the health facts, products, and services.** Decide which information is the most important to help keep yourself safe from harm.

LESSON REVIEW

Review Concepts

1. **List** three safety rules to follow when you run outdoors.

2. **Explain** how you can stay safe on the playground.

3. **Tell** why you should not use a telephone during a thunderstorm.

4. **Name** three rules to follow during a tornado.

Critical Thinking

5. **Plan** Suppose that you are at a playground and you see that a thunderstorm is coming. Describe the steps you would take to stay safe.

6. **LIFE SKILLS** **Access Health Facts, Products, and Services** Suppose that your community has very cold weather. How can you find out how to keep safe during this weather?

Set Health Goals

Problem Alex knows that he can get injured at the playground. He wants to set a goal to stay safe while playing.

Health Behavior Contract

Name _____   Date _____

Health Goal: I will follow safety rules at school and home.

Effect on My Health: I will stay safe from harm and injury if I follow safety rules.

My Plan: I will make a chart that lists the days of the week. I will track each safety rule for playground equipment that I follow. I will use the chart below to keep track of my progress. I will get help from my parents and my teacher.

Safety Rules	S	M	T	W	Th	F	S
I will make sure an adult is nearby.	✕			✕	✕		✕
I will not play on equipment that is broken.		✕		✕		✕	✕
I will only play on equipment with a soft surface underneath.			✕		✕	✕	✕

How My Plan Worked: My plan helped me to stay safe while playing on the playground. I followed all of the safety rules. I kept safe from injury and harm.

Solution Alex can figure out what goal he wants to set about playground safety. Then, he can make a plan to follow using the steps on page C59.

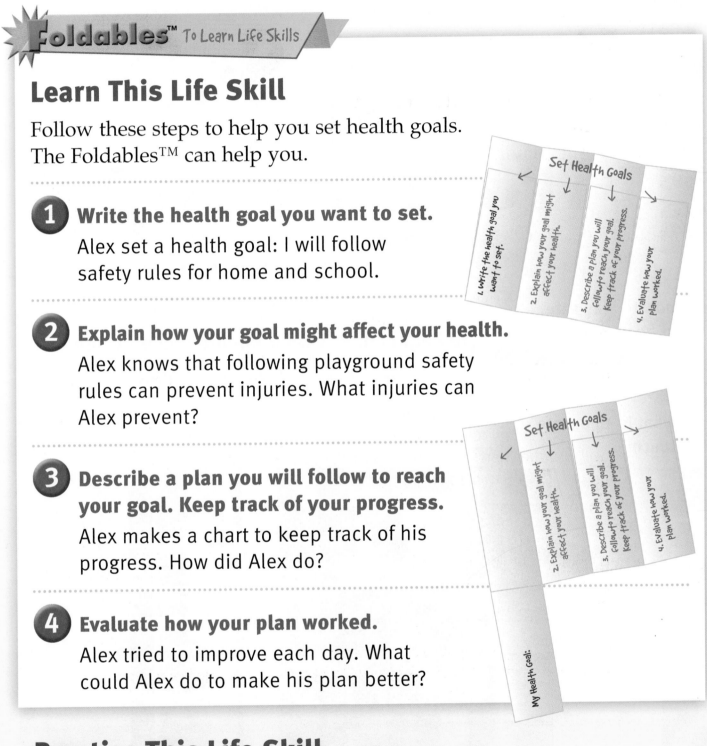

Learn This Life Skill

Follow these steps to help you set health goals.
The Foldables™ can help you.

1 **Write the health goal you want to set.**

Alex set a health goal: I will follow
safety rules for home and school.

2 **Explain how your goal might affect your health.**

Alex knows that following playground safety
rules can prevent injuries. What injuries can
Alex prevent?

3 **Describe a plan you will follow to reach
your goal. Keep track of your progress.**

Alex makes a chart to keep track of his
progress. How did Alex do?

4 **Evaluate how your plan worked.**

Alex tried to improve each day. What
could Alex do to make his plan better?

Practice This Life Skill

Role-play. Set a goal for following safety rules
when you play. Make a health behavior contract.

Staying Safe Around People

You will learn . . .

- how to stay safe at home.
- how to stay safe from strangers.
- what is an unsafe touch.

Vocabulary

- **violence**, *C61*
- **stranger**, *C62*
- **unsafe touch**, *C63*

You have friends you play with at school. Teachers and other trusted adults are there to help you. But what should you do when you meet strangers? You can follow rules to stay safe.

Keep Safe at Home

Sometimes your parents or guardian can't answer the phone or door. They might be busy cleaning or helping another family member. Or, someone might call your home and ask questions. Sometimes these people use violence to get what they want. **Violence** is harm done to yourself, others, or property. To keep yourself safe, follow these safety rules if someone comes to your home.

- **Keep the doors locked.** Stay inside.

- **Don't let anyone into your home.** Wait until your parents or guardian can come to the door. If you can't find your parents or guardian and the person won't go away, dial 9-1-1.

- **Don't give your name, address, or telephone number to someone on the telephone.** Do not answer any questions. Hang up the phone if the caller bothers you.

 What do you do if someone you do not know calls your home?

write About It!

Dialogue Look at the pictures below. Write sample dialogues like those you see in the pictures. Work with a partner to practice the situations and lines that you wrote.

Is your mother or father there? I have something important to ask them.

My mother can't get to the phone right now. Can I take a message?

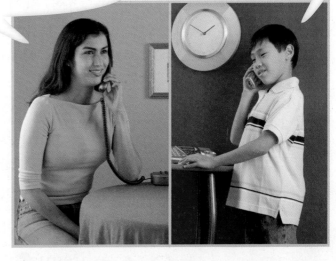

▲ Always tell a caller that your parents or guardian cannot come to the phone if they are busy.

Strangers and Your Safety

A **stranger** is someone you do not know well. Keep safe around strangers by following these rules.

- Do not play alone.
- Do not take candy, money, or toys from a stranger.
- Do not go near a stranger who wants to show you a pet.
- Never get into a car with a stranger.
- Do not go anywhere with a stranger, even if a stranger says that your parents or guardian said it's okay.

If a stranger bothers you, run away. Go to where there are other people, such as into a store. Yell so that people will know you are worried and will help. Tell your parents or guardian about a stranger who bothers you.

Who Can You Trust If You Are Lost?

If you are ever lost or don't know where you are, do not panic. Read the following list to see which people you can trust.

- An adult who works in a store
- A lifeguard if you are lost at the beach
- A teacher at your school
- A police officer or firefighter

ACTIVITY

Health Online

Amber Alert System

The Amber Alert system helps recover missing children across the United States. Research and report on how the Amber Alert system helps find missing children using the e-Journal writing tool. Visit **www.mmhhealth.com** and click on ⊕-Journal.

▲ **You can trust a teacher if you are lost.**

A Touch That Is Not Right

An **unsafe touch** is a touch that is wrong. It is not okay for anyone to touch your private body parts. To protect yourself, you can:

- **Tell** the person to stop touching you.
- **Run away** from this person.
- **Yell** as loud as you can.
- **Tell a responsible adult.** If the first adult you tell does not believe you, tell another adult.

 What is an unsafe touch?

LIFE SKILLS · **ACTIVITY**

CRITICAL THINKING

Use Resistance Skills

Act out a skit. A stranger comes to your door wearing a uniform. He asks to come in.

1. **Look at the person. Say "no" in a firm voice.** The uniformed man knocks on the door. The student says "no" when the uniformed man asks to come in.

2. **Give reasons for saying "no."** The student's parents are busy cleaning.

3. **Match your behavior to your words.** The student makes sure the door is locked and walks away.

4. **Ask an adult for help if you need it.** The uniformed man won't leave. The student uses the telephone to dial 9-1-1.

Students discuss the skit. They decide whether the student handled the uniformed man correctly.

LESSON REVIEW

Review Concepts

1. **Explain** what to do to keep safe if someone comes to the door of your home.

2. **List** three safety rules to stay safe from strangers who might want to harm you.

3. **Explain** how to protect yourself from an unsafe touch.

Critical Thinking

4. **Evaluate** You are waiting for your parent to pick you up after school. A person comes and says that your parent sent him to pick you up. Is it safe to go with the person? Explain.

5. **LIFE SKILLS** **Use Resistance Skills** Suppose that a stranger in a car asks you for help. How can you use resistance skills to keep safe?

Staying Safe From Violence

You will learn . . .

- ways that you can stay safe from a gang.

- why you should not pretend to have a weapon.

- what to do if you find a weapon.

Vocabulary

- **gang**, *C65*

- **weapon**, *C66*

Young people should make friends who are safe to be around. Friends should help each other practice healthful behaviors.

Gangs: What You Should Know

What do you know about gangs? A **gang** is a group of people involved in acts that are dangerous or against the law.

Gang members often wear certain colors or clothes. They might draw graffiti. Gang members act in violent ways. They often carry weapons, such as knives and guns. They sometimes use weapons to hurt people. Gang members often bully others to join or to obey. They might sell and use drugs, and rob other people. Gang members often fight members of other gangs.

 Why do some people join gangs?

BUILD ACTIVITY

Character
A Real Family

Caring Draw a cartoon about Joey. Joey is a young man who is in a gang. His friends convince him to leave the gang. Joey becomes closer to his real friends.

▶ **True friends care for one another.**

Weapons: Know What to Do

Write a Song Write a song about the importance of following safety rules and staying away from weapons. Read or sing your song for the class.

A **weapon** is an object that is used to harm someone. A weapon can be a gun, knife, or a baseball bat. A person might be harmed on purpose by someone with a weapon. Sometimes a person is around a weapon and is harmed by accident.

It is important to protect yourself from weapons. Follow these safety rules.

- **Do not touch or carry a weapon.** You could be accidentally injured.

- **Do not pretend to have a weapon.** Someone could harm you if they think you are threatening them.

- **Do not bring weapons or toy weapons to school.** It is illegal.

Weapons at Home

You might see a weapon in your home or a friend's home. Never touch the weapon. Talk to your parents or guardian about safe storage of weapons. A gun can be a weapon. It should be locked in a gun case. Guns should not be loaded. They should have triggers locked. Ammunition should be stored by itself.

 How should a gun be stored?

S.A.F.E.

If you see or find a weapon, think **S.A.F.E.**

S — Stop.

A — Avoid going near the weapon.

F — Find an adult.

E — Explain what you saw.

Analyze What Influences Your Health

Role-play a conversation between Arlene and Sammy about a knife in a drawer.

1. **Identify people and things that can influence your health.** Arlene shows the knife to Sammy. The class decides who is trying to influence Sammy.

2. **Evaluate how these people and things can affect your health.** Arlene asks Sammy if he wants to hold the knife.

3. **Choose healthful influences.** Sammy explains his decision to Arlene.

4. **Protect yourself against harmful influences.** The class discusses how Sammy can protect himself from harmful influences.

LESSON REVIEW

Review Concepts

1. **Analyze** how members of gangs act.

2. **Tell** why you should not pretend to have a weapon.

3. **Name** three rules that protect you from weapons.

4. **Explain** what the letters **S.A.F.E.** mean if you find a weapon.

Critical Thinking

5. **Decide** At school, your friend tells you that he has a weapon in his book bag. Decide what you should do. Tell why your friend is acting unsafe.

6. **LIFE SKILLS Analyze What Influences Your Health** Suppose that your older brother shows you a pocket knife. He asks you if you want to play with it. Evaluate how your brother is influencing your health.

Emergencies

You will learn . . .

- how to call for help in an emergency.
- how to help an injured person.
- what safety rules to follow in case of a disaster.

Vocabulary

- **emergency**, C69

Emergencies can happen anywhere at anytime. You could be at home during bad weather. You might be at school when someone trips and cuts his or her knee. You might be playing with your friends outside when someone gets injured. It is important to know what to do in case of an emergency.

What Is a Medical Emergency?

An **emergency** is a situation in which help is needed quickly. It could be caused by bad weather, a fire, or crime. A medical emergency is when someone's health has been harmed. The following situations are medical emergencies:

- breathing is hard or stops
- having a bad chest pain
- swallowing a poison
- bleeding that will not stop
- coughing or spitting up blood
- feeling very bad pain
- passing out

Use the steps listed at the right when you need to call for help.

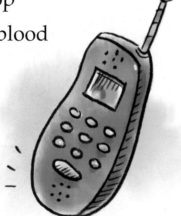

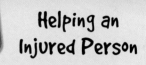

Helping an Injured Person

1. **Stay calm.** Try to think clearly.

2. **Stay safe.** Make sure the area around you is safe so that you do not injure yourself.

3. **Never** move an injured person.

4. **Get help fast!** Get an adult or tell someone to do so. Dial 9-1-1 if it is an emergency.

5. **Keep the person warm.** Use a blanket or jacket.

 What are the rules for helping a person who is injured?

Being Prepared

CAREERS

Emergency Medical Technician

An emergency medical technician (EMT) gives emergency medical care to people who are injured or suddenly ill. An EMT might respond to emergency calls, such as accidents. He or she might treat wounds, bleeding, broken bones, breathing problems, and heart attacks.

LOG ON www.mmhhealth.com Find out more about this and other health careers.

Do you know what to do during an emergency? You can make a disaster kit. Include first aid supplies, a flashlight, and a battery powered radio. You should also include food, water, and a plan for how to get in touch with family members in an emergency. Keep a list of phone numbers. If you need to call for help, dial 9-1-1. Tell what the emergency is. Give your name and the address where you are. Listen to what you are told to do. Stay on the phone until you are told to hang up.

▲ A family disaster kit is very important to have in case of a disaster.

Safety Drills

All schools have drills that they practice in case of disasters. Follow these safety rules during drills to protect yourself.

- **Know your alarm sounds** to recognize what the different alarm sounds mean.

- **Stay quiet.** Listen to your teacher's instructions.

- **Go to the place that your teacher and school have decided on.** Be orderly. Do not run.

 How can your family be prepared for a disaster?

Manage Stress

You are thinking about how to be safe in an emergency. You are feeling stress. What can you do? Work with a partner. Answer the questions below. Write your answers on the chalkboard.

1. **Identify the signs of stress.** What are the signs of stress you might have?

2. **Identify the cause of stress.** What types of emergencies might cause you stress?

3. **Do something about the cause of stress.** What can you do to relieve your stress?

4. **Take action to reduce the harmful effects of stress.** What action can you take to reduce the stress you feel about emergency situations?

LESSON REVIEW

Review Concepts

1. **Describe** three examples of times when you need to call for emergency medical help.

2. **Explain** what you should do to help yourself think clearly while helping an injured person.

3. **List** three items to include in a disaster kit.

Critical Thinking

4. **Analyze** Suppose that you want to have drills for natural disasters. Which natural disasters are likely to happen where you live? How do you know?

5. **LIFE SKILLS** **Manage Stress** You are having stress about what to do for your pet in case of a disaster. What can you do to manage your stress?

How to Give First Aid

You will learn . . .

- what precautions to take when giving first aid.

- how to give first aid for cuts, scrapes, nosebleeds, bruises, burns, insect stings, animal bites, reactions to poisonous plants, and choking.

- what items should be part of a first aid kit.

Vocabulary

- **first aid**, *C73*
- **first aid kit**, *C77*

A person who is injured might need your help. He might have a cut on his elbow. Maybe she has an insect bite on her arm. You can use first aid to help improve a person's health.

What Is First Aid?

Sometimes people have accidents. They might fall on the cement and scrape their knees. They might burn their finger on the stove. Maybe they stub their toe on a chair. These injuries are minor injuries. They can be treated by giving first aid. **First aid** is the quick care given to a person who is injured or is suddenly ill. You can use first aid steps to treat many minor injuries. There are some steps you should always follow when you perform first aid.

Follow these steps when performing first aid to protect yourself.

1. **Do not touch someone else's blood.** You could get someone else's germs or give your germs to someone else.

2. **Wash your hands with soap and water after giving first aid.**

3. **Do not eat or drink while giving first aid.**

4. **Do not touch your mouth, eyes, or nose while giving first aid.**

5. **Ask an adult if you need help.**

Why should you avoid touching someone else's blood?

On Your Own
FOR SCHOOL OR HOME

Emergency Telephone Numbers

If someone gets injured and needs emergency care, every second counts. Having a list of telephone numbers can save time. Make a list of emergency and important telephone numbers to post by the phone. Include your home address so that it is handy.

EMERGENCY TELEPHONE NUMBERS

3747 Maple Drive

Mom at Work: 555-3829
Dad at Work: 555-8593
Grandma: 555-7075
Aunt Kathy: 222-0536
Police Station: 555-1954
Fire Station: 555-7462
OTHER: 9-1-1

Steps in Giving First Aid

Minor cuts, scrapes, burns, and bruises are minor injuries. Many injuries can be treated with first aid. Follow these steps when treating injuries.

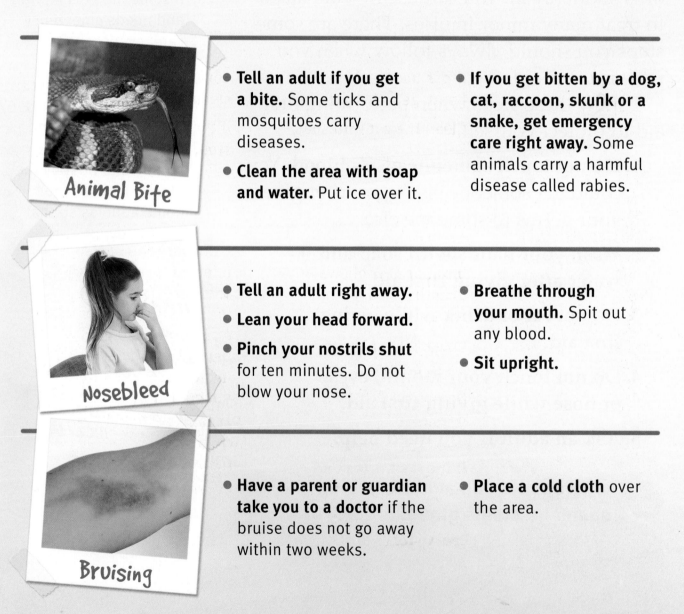

Animal Bite

- **Tell an adult if you get a bite.** Some ticks and mosquitoes carry diseases.
- **Clean the area with soap and water.** Put ice over it.
- **If you get bitten by a dog, cat, raccoon, skunk or a snake, get emergency care right away.** Some animals carry a harmful disease called rabies.

Nosebleed

- **Tell an adult right away.**
- **Lean your head forward.**
- **Pinch your nostrils shut** for ten minutes. Do not blow your nose.
- **Breathe through your mouth.** Spit out any blood.
- **Sit upright.**

Bruising

- **Have a parent or guardian take you to a doctor** if the bruise does not go away within two weeks.
- **Place a cold cloth** over the area.

Sting

- **Tell an adult if you get a sting.** If the insect has a disease or poison, you will need emergency care.

- **If you get a sting, have an adult remove the stinger.** Scrape it out with a hard card or a clean nail file. Do not squeeze it out.

- **Clean the area with soap and water.** Put ice over it.

- **If you can't breathe, if you feel dizzy, or if the area swells,** get emergency care right away.

Cuts and Scrapes

- **Press on the cut** with a bandage if the cut bleeds.

- **Clean the cut** with soap and water.

- **Cover the cut** with a clean bandage.

- **If the bleeding does not stop,** get a responsible adult or dial 9-1-1.

Burn

- **Put a cold cloth over the burn,** or run cold water over the burn for 10 minutes.

- **Cover the burn** with a clean bandage.

- **Do not break** a blister or bubble.

- **If the burn or a blister gets infected,** see a doctor. There are signs to look for if a blister is infected. An infected blister may become warm or swell up. It may become redder or the fluid may drain. It may become more painful.

Rash

- **If the rash is in or near your eyes,** see a doctor.

- **Use calamine lotion or cool water** to treat the rash.

- **Do not scratch or rub** the rash.

- **Run cold water** over the area.

 What are the first aid steps for a burn?

Choking

Sometimes a person may choke while eating. Chew your food slowly. Don't talk while you are chewing and swallowing. Remain seated. Don't eat and run. Be careful when eating certain foods that can get stuck in your throat, such as hot dogs and candies.

If someone is choking, follow these steps when giving first aid. You should be trained to do this before you try it.

1. **Ask the person, "Are you choking?"** The person might nod or make the sign for choking.

2. **Stand behind the person.**

3. **Wrap your arms around the person's waist.**

4. **Make a fist with one hand and grasp your fist with the other.** Press into the person's stomach just above their navel. Use quick, upward pushes. Don't press so hard that you break or injure the person's ribs.

5. **Give pushes until the food comes out.** Tell someone to dial 9-1-1 if the person does not stop choking.

 What is the sign for someone who is choking?

▲ This is the universal choking sign. Make this sign if you are choking.

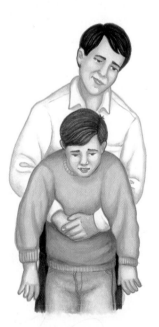

▲ Stand behind the person who is choking. Use quick, upward pushes into the stomach, just above the navel.

Filling a First Aid Kit

A **first aid kit** is a collection of supplies used to care for a person who is injured or ill. Supplies include:

- gauze pads
- adhesive bandages
- towelettes
- scissors
- tweezers
- adhesive tape
- gauze roller bandages
- directions for emergency help

ACTIVITY

LIFE SKILLS

CRITICAL THINKING

Be a Health Advocate

1. **Choose a healthful action to communicate.** What is the healthful action? You want to teach people about first aid.

2. **Collect information about the action.** Use your textbook to find information about first aid for cuts and scrapes.

3. **Decide how to communicate this information.** You might design a first aid brochure. Have one page for each type of first aid.

4. **Communicate your message to others.** Present your brochure to the class.

LESSON REVIEW

Review Concepts

1. **Explain** why you should not touch someone's blood while giving first aid.

2. **List** the first aid steps for a bruise.

3. **Name** four items often found in a first aid kit.

Critical Thinking

4. **Apply** Draw a picture of how to give first aid to a person who is choking. Use words to describe what to do.

5. **LIFE SKILLS** **Be a Health Advocate** You find out that only a few of the people you know have first aid kits at home. How can you get more of them to have first aid kits?

CHAPTER 6 REVIEW

Use Vocabulary

accident, *C43*

emergency, *C69*

first aid kit, *C77*

personal flotation device, *C52*

thunderstorm, *C56*

violence, *C61*

Choose the correct term from the list to complete each sentence.

1. Supplies that are needed to give first aid, such as gauze pads and adhesive bandages, are found in a(n) __?__.

2. Someone is having a hard time breathing. You should call for help quickly. This situation is a(n) __?__.

3. Never go near a stranger. A stranger could harm you. Harm done to yourself, others, or property is called __?__.

4. In order to protect yourself during a(n) __?__, which is a storm with thunder and lightning, keep away from water.

5. If you are riding in a boat, you should always wear an object that helps you stay afloat in water called a(n) __?__.

6. Something that is not supposed to happen is called a(n) __?__.

Review Concepts

Answer each question in complete sentences.

7. Name a hazard that might make you fall at home. Tell how you can keep safe in this example.

8. Explain how you can stay safe on a playground.

9. Describe the safe way to wait for a school bus.

10. Explain what to do if someone touches you in a way that is wrong.

11. Explain why gangs can be dangerous.

Reading Comprehension

Answer each question in complete sentences.

- **Have your parents check smoke alarm batteries.** Smoke alarm batteries should be checked at least twice a year.

- **Call for help if you see a fire.** Dial 9-1-1.

12. Tell who you should ask to check smoke alarm batteries.

13. Identify how many times smoke alarm batteries should be checked.

14. Name the number you should dial if you see a fire.

Critical Thinking/Problem Solving

Answer each question in complete sentences.

Analyze Concepts

15. You and your parents decide to ride bicycles down the road. Tell how you would signal a left turn.

16. You are planning to give a talk to first graders about ways to prevent choking. What information will you include in your speech?

17. During a game of street hockey, your friend falls and hurts his knee. His knee turns black and blue. Decide what type of injury your friend has. List the first aid steps for treating it.

18. When you get home from school, your parents are busy cleaning the attic. Describe what you should do to keep yourself safe if someone comes to the door.

19. At school, your class practiced what to do in case of a tornado. Describe the practice session.

20. What should you do if you get lost at a shopping mall?

Practice Life Skills

21. **Set Health Goals** Set a health goal to follow safety rules while riding in a car. Explain how this might affect your health.

22. **Make Responsible Decisions** You see a weapon on the playground at school. What should you do? Identify the responsible decision.

Read Graphics

The table shows first aid steps for a cut and a rash. Use the table to answer questions 23–24.

First Aid for Cuts

Injury	Steps
Cut	• Clean the cut with soap and water. • Cover the cut with a clean bandage.
Rash	• Run cold water over the area. • Do not scratch or rub the rash.

23. Describe how to clean a cut.

24. Identify what to run over a rash.

 LOG ON www.mmhhealth.com Find out more about preventing violence and injury.

Effective Communication

Write a Skit

Write a skit. Two friends are on opposite football teams. One friend begins yelling and pushes the other friend. Include how the two friends can be good sports towards one another.

Self-Directed Learning

Follow Directions

Write the directions from your shampoo bottle on the left side of a two-column chart. Write how you wash your hair on the right. Compare both sides. Correct any steps that do not match.

Critical Thinking and Problem Solving

Electrical Safety

You want to plug your television, alarm clock, and lamp into one outlet. Explain why this is an unsafe situation. Decide which ones you could do without.

Responsible Citizenship

Design a Sign

Design signs to hang up outside on the playground at your school. The signs should have safety rules that everyone should follow in order to stay safe.

Medicine and You

The adult in the photo is giving his child cough medicine. Cough medicine is a drug. A **drug** is a substance, other than food, that changes how your mind or body works. The parent is giving his daughter the medicine to help her stop coughing.

Medicines are drugs used to treat, prevent, or cure an illness or injury. Medicines can be helpful when used safely. Medicines can relieve a cough, heal burned skin, stop a runny nose, and prevent disease. Medicines come in many forms.

- **Tablets** These are swallowed with water.

- **Creams** Creams, such as ointments or lotions, are placed on your skin to clear up rashes.

- **Spray** Liquid medicine can be sprayed into your nose or mouth or onto your skin.

- **Injections** Medicines can be put into your body using a needle.

Medicines can be bought at drugstores. They are legal drugs. Legal drugs are safe when used as directed. Some drugs are illegal. They are not safe to use. Illegal drugs can harm your body. Say "no" to illegal drugs.

 How do medicines help people?

Consumer Wise
ACTIVITY

Comparing Prices

Go with your parent or guardian to a drugstore. Find two bottles of cough syrup. One bottle should be a brand name. The other bottle should be generic. Compare prices of each bottle. Which cough syrup is cheaper? How much cheaper? Which one would you buy?

▲ **Medicines can help you feel better when they are used correctly.**

Two Kinds of Medicines

CAREERS

Pharmacist

A pharmacist has a bachelor's degree and an advanced degree. He or she then has to pass a test to receive a license. A licensed pharmacist fills prescriptions written by doctors. Pharmacists work in drugstores, hospitals, and grocery stores. They also work for companies that make drugs.

 LOG ON www.mmhhealth.com
Find out more about other health careers.

A doctor might give you medicine when you are ill. He or she writes you an order for a prescription (prih•SKRIP•shuhn). **Prescription medicine** is medicine that your doctor writes an order for. Your parents or guardian can buy it at a drugstore. A pharmacist (FAHR•muh•sist) can fill the doctor's order for the medicine. No one else should take your prescribed medicine but you.

Over-the-counter (OTC) medicines are medicines adults can buy without a doctor's written order. These medicines may be used to treat a headache, upset stomach, cold, or body pain. Your parent or guardian will read the directions on the bottle. The directions tell the safe way to use the drug.

 Name the two kinds of medicines.

Some OTC Medicines

Drug	How It Helps Health
Cough Medicine	Helps control coughs
Antibiotic (ant•ee•bigh•OT•tik) Ointment	Helps kill germs in cuts and scrapes
Allergy (AL•luhr•jee) Medicine	Helps relieve itchy eyes and runny noses

Medicine Labels

Medicines have labels. Each label has important information you should know. Read all medicine labels with your parents or guardian. Study the labels on this page.

BEST DRUG STORE Rx
150 SUNSHINE LANE   NEW BOSTON, NH 03070

MR. PAUL SCOTT
1030 Hillcrest Ave
New Boston, NH 03070

TAKE 1 TABLET
EVERY 8 HOURS
Penicillin 200 mg
EXP: 7/30
Dr. Mark Smith

Directions Your parents or guardian will follow the directions on the prescription correctly. Never take medicine from anyone but your parents or guardian. Never take it on your own.

Dosage Always take the correct amount of medicine.

Name Never take prescription medicine that is prescribed for someone else. Be sure your name is on the label.

OTC Labels

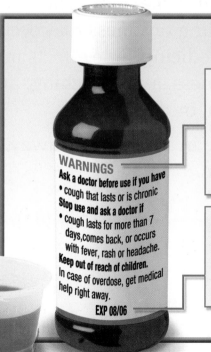

WARNINGS
Ask a doctor before use if you have
• Cough that lasts or is chronic
Stop use and ask a doctor if
• Cough lasts for more than 7 days, comes back, or occurs with fever, rash or headache.
Keep out of reach of children.
In case of overdose, get medical help right away.

EXP 08/06

Warnings Your parents or guardian will read the warning label on the back of OTC medicines. The label tells who should not take the medicine. Some people are allergic to medicine.

Expiration Date Never take medicine that has passed the expiration date. An adult should get rid of expired medicine in a safe way.

Using Medicine Safely

Never take medicine unless given to you by a responsible adult such as your parent or guardian or your school nurse. It also is important to follow safety rules when taking medicine.

- Follow the directions on the label.

- Take all the medicine that a doctor prescribes. Do not use medicine that has passed the expiration date.

- Check the safety seal on OTC medicines before buying. Make sure it is not broken. Do not buy OTC medicines if the seal is broken.

- Tell an adult if you have a side effect from taking medicine. A *side effect* is an unwanted feeling or illness that occurs after taking medicine. Side effects may include sleepiness, a rash, itching, an upset stomach, or dizziness.

- Keep medicine in a safe place, away from young children.

 Name the person who should give you your medicine.

Unsafe Use of Drugs

Drug misuse is the unsafe use of medicine taken by accident. For example, a person can take 3 teaspoons of medicine instead of 2 by mistake. You can prevent drug misuse by following the safety rules for taking medicines.

Drug abuse is the unsafe use of a medicine or an illegal drug on purpose. *Illegal* means against the law. For example, a person may have a prescription drug for headaches. The label on the drug reads, "Take one tablet a day." The person decides to take two or more tablets a day. This is drug abuse.

LESSON REVIEW

Review Concepts

1. **Explain** ways medicines can help health.

2. **Compare** the two kinds of medicines.

3. **List** three safety rules for using medicine.

Critical Thinking

4. **Apply** You have an upset stomach. Your friend offers you his or her prescription drug. What should you do? Explain your answer.

5. **LIFE SKILLS** **Be a Health Advocate** What steps can you follow to be a health advocate for the safe use of medicines?

Alcohol

You will learn . . .

- ways that alcohol affects physical health.

- ways that alcohol affects how a person thinks, feels, and acts.

- ways to say "no" to drinking alcohol.

Vocabulary

- **alcohol**, *D11*

This boy and girl are having fun. They have good health. Drinking alcohol can harm health. Say "no" to drinking alcohol.

Alcohol Affects Physical Health

Alcohol is a drug that slows down the mind and the body. It is found in some drinks. When a person drinks alcohol, it quickly enters the blood. The blood carries the alcohol to all parts of the body. The drawing below shows the different parts of the body affected by alcohol.

 What is alcohol?

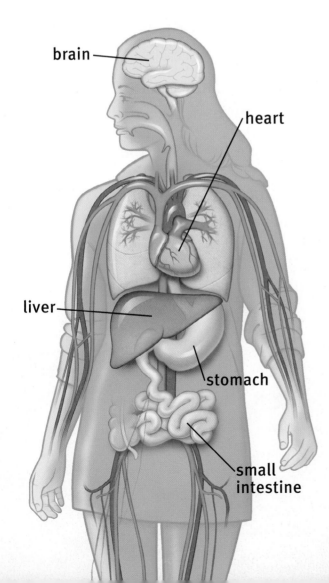

brain

heart

liver

stomach

small intestine

How Alcohol Affects the Body

- **Brain** Alcohol slows down the way the brain works. A person can't think clearly or react correctly to messages the body sends to the brain.

- **Heart** Heavy drinking can cause heart failure.

- **Liver** Too much alcohol can harm the liver.

- **Stomach** Too much alcohol can harm stomach cells.

- **Small Intestine** Too much alcohol can harm the small intestine and cause digestion problems.

- **Senses** Alcohol dulls the senses of sight, hearing, smell, touch, and taste.

Alcohol Changes the Way People Act

The brain is the control center of the body. A person who drinks alcohol might not be in control of what he or she does. The person might not be alert, or ready to act. When drinking alcohol, people often

- make wrong decisions.
- say things that hurt other people's feelings.
- forget things they already have learned.
- become angry and get into fights when there is a conflict.
- are unable to walk and talk properly because they cannot control their muscles.
- become sad.

▼ Drinking alcohol and driving is against the law. It can lead to car crashes.

ACTIVITY

Physical Education LINK

IT Alert

Test your alertness. Play this game with a group of six or more. Choose one player to be IT. The rest of the group will stand in a circle around IT. Give every player a number, including IT. Call out two numbers. The players whose numbers are called must try to change places. IT tries to move into an open space before either player gets there. The player who is left out will be the new IT.

Drinking Alcohol Can Harm Others

People who drink alcohol can harm themselves and others. Here are three ways others could be harmed.

- **Drinking alcohol can cause accidents.** People can do dangerous things like driving after drinking. Drinking and then driving causes accidents.

- **Drinking alcohol can cause crime and violence.** People who drink alcohol aren't able to make responsible decisions. They may show their feelings in ways that harm others.

- **Drinking alcohol can cause problems in a family.** Family members who drink often are not as dependable or responsible as those who don't drink. They might forget a family function.

 What are three ways that drinking alcohol can change the way people act?

Science LINK

ACTIVITY

Learning with Balloons!

You will need a red and blue balloon for this activity. The red balloon represents a healthy stomach. The blue balloon represents a stomach damaged by alcohol. With your teacher, use a paper clip to poke holes through the blue balloon. Now fill both balloons with water over the sink. Describe what happened. How is the blue balloon different from the red one?

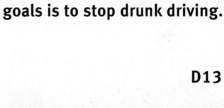

Too Young to DIE

Face the Truth about Underage Drinking

MADD

Mothers Against Drunk D...

◀ **MADD stands for *Mothers Against Drunk Driving*. MADD is an organization that educates young people and adults about the dangers of alcohol. One of MADD's goals is to stop drunk driving.**

Say "No" to Alcohol

You can use resistance skills if someone pressures you to drink alcohol.

1. **Look at the person. Say "no" in a firm voice.**

2. **Give reasons for saying "no."**

   - I want to protect my health and keep my mind clear.
   - I want to be safe and avoid accidents.
   - I want to follow rules and laws.
   - I want to show respect in my relationships.
   - I want to follow my family guidelines.
   - I want to be alcohol free and show good character.

3. **Match your behavior with your words.** Walk away if someone wants you to drink.

4. **Ask an adult for help if you need it.** Tell your parents or guardians what happened. They will help you stick to your no.

 What are two reasons to say "no" to alcohol?

▲ Say "no" to alcohol, and stay safe.

Use Communication Skills

Role-play a conversation between Alice and Tina. Alice wants to make a poster to teach students about the harmful effects of alcohol. Tina does not feel that sharing health facts is important.

1 **Choose the best way to communicate.** Alice will remember to use good communication skills.

2 **Send a clear message. Be polite.** What should Alice say to Tina? How can she tell her that sharing healthful facts is important?

3 **Listen to each other.** How can Tina let Alice know that she is listening? How can Alice let Tina know that she is listening?

4 **Make sure you understand each other.** How should Tina let Alice know that she understands her?

LESSON REVIEW

Review Concepts

1. **List** three ways that alcohol harms physical health.

2. **Describe** how alcohol affects relationships.

3. **List** the steps to follow to say "no" if someone asks you to drink alcohol.

Critical Thinking

4. **Apply** Create a poster that will tell people how drinking alcohol can harm others. What should the poster say?

5. **LIFE SKILLS** **Use Communication Skills** Your friend's teenage brother wants to know if you want a ride home from school. You and your friend see an open can of beer in his car. What should you do?

D15

Tobacco

You will learn . . .

- how smoking and smokeless tobacco harm health.
- ways secondhand tobacco smoke harms health.
- ways ads try to get people to use tobacco.
- ways to say "no" to tobacco use.

Vocabulary

- **tobacco**, *D17*
- **nicotine**, *D17*
- **dependence**, *D17*
- **secondhand smoke**, *D18*

Cigarettes are a tobacco product. They contain harmful chemicals. There are over 4,000 harmful chemicals in tobacco smoke. Many buildings have no smoking signs. This helps to keep the environment in the building healthy.

Tobacco Has Harmful Chemicals

Tobacco is a plant. Tobacco is found in cigarettes, cigars, pipe tobacco, and chewing tobacco. It contains many harmful chemicals, like nicotine.

Nicotine (NI•kuh•TEEN) is a drug found in tobacco. It speeds up your body. It makes your heart beat faster, for example. People who use tobacco can develop a dependence on nicotine. **Dependence** is a strong need for something. Once someone has nicotine dependence, it becomes harder to quit using tobacco. Over time, tobacco use can harm many parts of your body. Look at the diagram below.

 What does having a dependence on a drug mean?

Ways Chemicals in Tobacco Can Harm Health

- **Face** Causes wrinkles and makes you look older.
- **Mouth** Causes gum disease and cancer.
- **Throat** Can cause throat cancer.
- **Lungs** Can cause frequent colds and lung disease.
- **Heart** Can cause high blood pressure and heart disease.
- **Stomach** Can cause stomach cancer and ulcers.

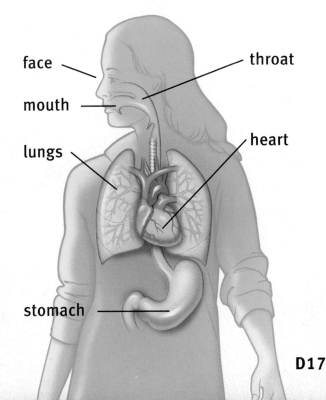

face

throat

mouth

heart

lungs

stomach

Secondhand Smoke

Have you ever been in a room where people were smoking? If you have, then you were breathing secondhand smoke. **Secondhand smoke** is the smoke that a smoker breathes out. It also is the smoke from a burning cigarette, cigar, or pipe. Secondhand smoke can make your eyes water and itch. It can make you cough. Over time it can even cause heart disease, lung cancer, and breathing problems.

You and your family should avoid secondhand smoke whenever possible. You can ask to sit in the nonsmoking section in restaurants, for example.

How can secondhand smoke harm you?

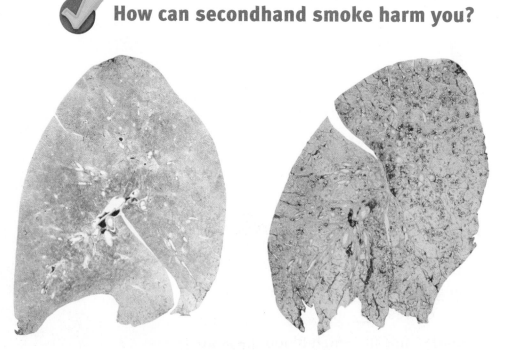

▲ Inhaling tobacco smoke damages the lungs. The lung on the left is from a person who did not smoke. The lung on the right has been damaged by smoking. What difference do you see?

Tobacco Ads

Tobacco companies advertise their products in magazines, on billboards, at sporting events, and at concerts. The companies advertise to get people to buy cigarettes, cigars, and chewing tobacco. But the law says tobacco ads must warn people that tobacco harms health. The warnings say that cigarette smoke has harmful gases that can cause disease.

✓ **Explain why a tobacco ad might show a group of people smoking.**

▼ **The pictures below show how tobacco companies try to sell products. What messages are the ads sending to consumers?**

How Tobacco Companies Advertise

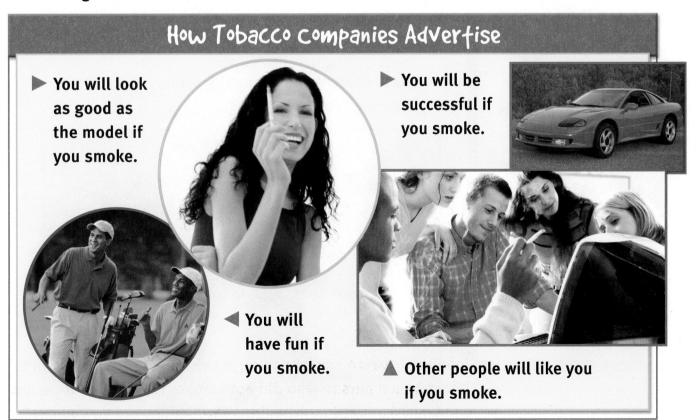

▶ You will look as good as the model if you smoke.

▶ You will be successful if you smoke.

◀ You will have fun if you smoke.

▲ Other people will like you if you smoke.

Say "No" To Tobacco

Use Resistance Skills

1. **Look at the person. Say "no" in a firm voice.**

2. **Give reasons for saying "no."**

3. **Match your behavior to your words.**

4. **Ask an adult for help if you need it.**

Guidelines for Making Responsible Decisions™

to say no to smoking:

- **Is it healthful? No.**

- **Is it safe? No.**

- **Does it follow rules and laws? No.**

- **Does it show respect for me and others? No**

- **Does it follow family guidelines? No.**

- **Does it show good character? No.**

Remember one word when someone offers you tobacco. The word is "no." You know that using tobacco is harmful to your health. It is also illegal for young people under the age of 18 to purchase tobacco.

Think of the diagram of the human body in this lesson. Think of all the parts of your body that tobacco can harm. Decide now that you will not use tobacco.

Sometimes a friend or an older student might offer you a cigarette. Tell him or her that you will not use tobacco. You want to live tobacco-free. Stand up for good health and help your friends decide to say "no."

▼ **These students have healthy smiles. They say "no" to smoking.**

Access Health Facts, Products, and Services

1 **Identify when you might need health facts, products, and services.** How might learning about the harmful effects of tobacco help you?

2 **Identify where you might find health facts, products, and services.** This textbook has lots of information on the harmful effects of tobacco. What other resources might help you?

3 **Find the health facts, products, and services you need.** Gather information about the harmful effects of smoking and make flash cards.

4 **Evaluate the health facts, products, and services.** Ask the school nurse or your family doctor for other facts that you should include on your cards.

What should you do if someone offers you tobacco?

LESSON REVIEW

Review Concepts

1. **Explain** what nicotine is and how it harms the body.

2. **Define** secondhand smoke.

3. **Tell** what you can say to a person who offers you a cigarette.

Critical Thinking

4. **Examine** Discuss what you should look for in tobacco advertisements.

5. **LIFE SKILLS** **Access Health Facts, Products, and Services**
A family member smokes. He or she gets upset when others suggest quitting. What should you do?

Use Resistance Skills

Problem Some older students are pressuring you to take just one puff from a cigarette. How can you use resistance skills to say "no"?

Solution Saying "no" to smoking a cigarette is a responsible decision. Use the steps on the next page to practice how to say "no."

Foldables™ To Learn Life Skills

Learn This Life Skill

Follow these steps to use resistance skills.
The Foldables™ can help you.

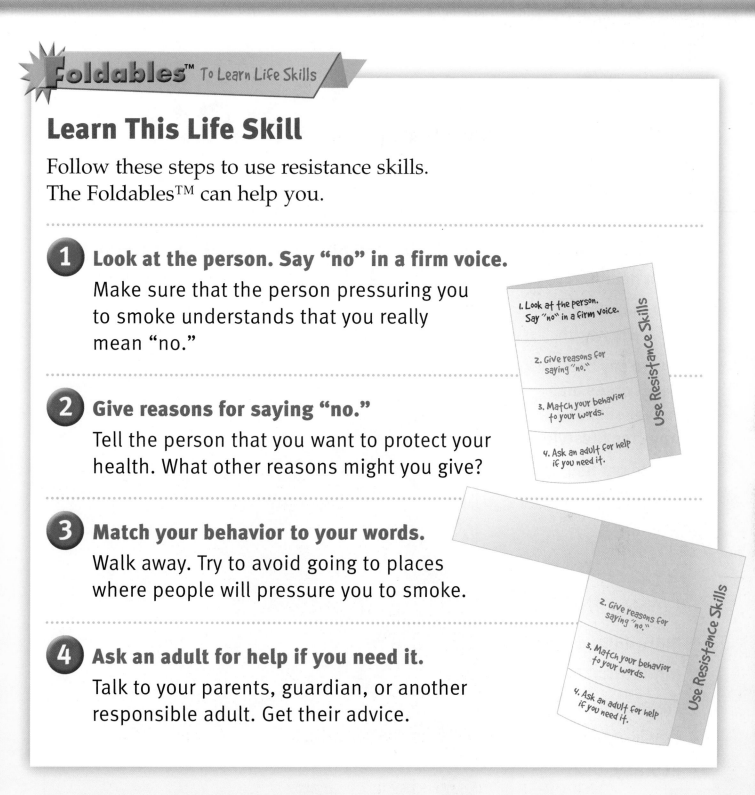

1 **Look at the person. Say "no" in a firm voice.**

Make sure that the person pressuring you to smoke understands that you really mean "no."

2 **Give reasons for saying "no."**

Tell the person that you want to protect your health. What other reasons might you give?

3 **Match your behavior to your words.**

Walk away. Try to avoid going to places where people will pressure you to smoke.

4 **Ask an adult for help if you need it.**

Talk to your parents, guardian, or another responsible adult. Get their advice.

Practice This Life Skill

With your classmates, role-play the situation above. Use the steps for using resistance skills.

Other Drugs

You will learn . . .

- ways caffeine can harm health.
- how illegal drug use can harm health.
- how to say "no" to illegal drugs and the benefits of a drug-free lifestyle.
- how to get help for drug abuse.

Vocabulary

- **caffeine**, *D25*
- **marijuana**, *D26*
- **inhalant**, *D26*
- **cocaine**, *D27*
- **crack**, *D27*
- **ecstasy**, *D27*

Drugs can be found in foods and drinks, like chocolate and soft drinks. You can choose to limit or avoid these foods and drinks.

Caffeine Affects the Mind and Body

Caffeine (kaf•EEN) is a drug that speeds up body actions. It can be found in some colas, coffee, tea, and chocolate. Caffeine changes how your mind or body works. Here are some examples of what caffeine can do to you:

- Your heart beats faster.
- You might feel nervous or shaky.
- You might feel more awake.
- You might get an upset stomach.

Some products say "decaffeinated," "no caffeine," or "caffeine-free." Choose these products. Or choose water, milk, or fruit juice. These drinks provide nutrients that help your body grow. They do not contain caffeine.

 Why is caffeine a drug?

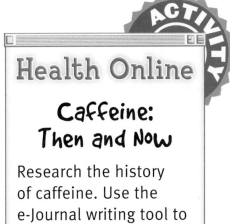

Health Online

Caffeine: Then and Now

Research the history of caffeine. Use the e-Journal writing tool to write your report. Visit **www.mmhhealth.com** and click on **e-Journal**.

ACTIVITY

▶ **Look for the words "caffeine-free" when choosing a cola to drink.**

Harmful Effects of Illegal Drugs

Some drugs are illegal. This means that it is against the law to buy, sell, or use these drugs. It is never safe to use an illegal drug.

Say "No" to Marijuana

Marijuana (mayr•uh•WAH•nuh) is an illegal drug that contains harmful chemicals. People who use marijuana get confused and find it hard to think. Smoking marijuana can harm the lungs and heart, just as smoking cigarettes can.

Say "No" to Inhalants

An **inhalant** (in•HAY•luhnt) is a chemical that is breathed into the lungs. Some inhalants are medicines. A doctor writes an order for these medicines.

Other inhalants are fumes that can come from materials like glue, spray paint, and gasoline.

Never breathe in these fumes on purpose. They can cause headaches, nosebleeds, brain damage, and death. Always read the warnings on the labels. Have your parents or guardian read the warnings with you. Open a window to get fresh air.

▼ It is important to read warning labels when using products that give off fumes.

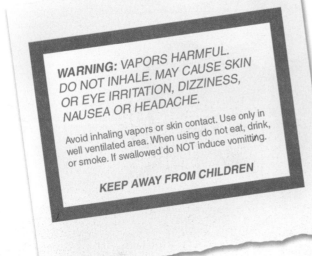

WARNING: VAPORS HARMFUL. DO NOT INHALE. MAY CAUSE SKIN OR EYE IRRITATION, DIZZINESS, NAUSEA OR HEADACHE.

Avoid inhaling vapors or skin contact. Use only in well ventilated area. When using do not eat, drink, or smoke. If swallowed do NOT induce vomiting.

KEEP AWAY FROM CHILDREN

Other Illegal Drugs

Cocaine (koh•KAYN) is an illegal drug that is made from the coca plant. It is a white powder. People who use cocaine inhale or inject it. Even young people can have heart attacks and die from using this drug.

Crack is an illegal drug that is a form of cocaine. This illegal drug is smoked. It affects the body in seconds.

Another illegal drug is ecstasy (EK•stuh•see). **Ecstasy** speeds up what happens inside the body. This drug is swallowed as a tablet or capsule. It also can be inhaled as a powder. Ecstasy can cause fainting, confusion, and brain damage.

What is an illegal drug?

▼ Choose a drug-free life. It is one of the most healthful choices you can make.

BUILD Character

Pledge to Be Drug-Free

Citizenship Write "I Pledge to Be Drug-Free" at the top of a sheet of paper. Then write the benefits of being drug-free. Sign your name and write the date at the bottom.

To be drug-free is to:

- Keep my body healthy
- Follow laws
- Show good character
- Keep friendships
- Get good grades
- Stay out of fights
- Keep my mind alert
- Avoid accidents and injuries

▶ **Always say "no" to drugs.**

Say "No" to Drugs

You can use resistance skills if someone pressures you to use drugs.

1. **Look at the person. Say "no" in a firm voice.**

2. **Give reasons for saying "no."**

   - I want to protect my health and keep my mind clear.
   - I want to follow rules and laws.
   - I want to show good character.

3. **Match your behavior with your words.** Walk away if someone wants you to use drugs.

4. **Ask an adult for help if you need it.** Tell your parents or guardian what happened. They will help you stick to your no.

✓ **What adults can you turn to for help when you say "no" to drugs?**

Getting Help for Drug Abuse

A person can get "hooked" on some drugs very quickly. It can be hard for this person to stop using drugs.

A person who can't stop taking a drug needs help. The person can talk to a doctor or counselor about different programs that help people to recover. Tell your parents, guardian, or another responsible adult if you know someone who is abusing drugs.

LESSON REVIEW

Review Concepts

1. **Discuss** two ways that caffeine can affect the mind and body.

2. **Explain** why marijuana and cocaine are illegal. Give two ways they can harm health.

3. **Identify** what you should do if you use a product that produces fumes.

Critical Thinking

4. **Identify** Name two benefits of a drug-free lifestyle.

5. **LIFE SKILLS** **Make Responsible Decisions** A classmate pressures you to smoke marijuana with him. What is the responsible decision for you to make?

CHAPTER 7 REVIEW

Use Vocabulary

alcohol, *D11*

caffeine, *D25*

dependence, *D17*

drug, *D5*

drug misuse, *D9*

nicotine, *D17*

over-the-counter
medicine (OTC), *D6*

Choose the correct term from the list to complete each sentence.

1. A drug that speeds up body actions is called __?__.

2. When a substance other than food changes how your mind or body works, it is called a __?__.

3. Medicine that adults can buy without a doctor's written order is called a(n) __?__.

4. A drug found in tobacco that speeds up the body is called __?__.

5. A drug that slows down your mind and body is called __?__.

6. The unsafe use of medicine taken by accident is called __?__.

7. A strong need for something is called __?__.

Review Concepts

Answer each question in complete sentences.

8. What are three forms in which medicine might be given to you?

9. List two ways that alcohol might change the way a person feels.

10. Name the one thing that every tobacco advertisement must show.

11. Describe what happens when a person gets "hooked" on drugs.

12. Tell two places that OTC drugs can be purchased by an adult.

Reading Comprehension

Answer each question in complete sentences.

An **inhalant** (in•HAY•luhnt) is a chemical that is breathed into the lungs. Some inhalants are medicine. They can be used if a doctor prescribes them.

Other inhalants are fumes that can come from glue, spray paint and gasoline.

13. Define an inhalant.

14. Identify three types of inhalants.

15. Explain when an inhalant might be used to help health.

Critical Thinking/Problem Solving

Answer each question in complete sentences.

Analyze Concepts

17. Your uncle drinks alcohol, smokes cigarettes, and never exercises. Explain why your uncle may have a greater chance of getting a chronic disease.

18. At school, your body begins to ache and you are coughing a lot. Explain how your body reacts to these types of symptoms.

19. Your grandmother has a cat. When you visit your grandmother, your eyes itch and water and your nose runs. Analyze why your body might react this way.

20. Your parents take you to the health department for a flu shot. Explain how the vaccine will help your body avoid the flu.

21. A classmate always has an assistant with her who uses sign language. Define what condition your classmate has and whether or not it is communicable.

Practice Life Skills

22. **Practice Healthful Behaviors** You have decided to practice behaviors to reduce your risk of cancer. Describe the behaviors you will make habits. Explain your choices.

23. **Make Responsible Decisions** Your friend has a cold. She wants you to play games with her. What is the responsible decision?

Read Graphics

The table describes a communicable disease common in children. Use it to answer questions 24–26.

A Communicable Disease

Disease	Symptoms	Cause	How Spread
Flu	Fever, cough, head and body aches, decreased appetite	Virus	In air (droplets released in coughs/sneezes), hands, and touching objects that have germs on them

24. Name the disease that is caused by a virus.

25. Identify two symptoms of the disease caused by a virus.

26. Explain how the disease is spread.

 LOG ON www.mmhhealth.com Find out more about communicable and chronic diseases.

Effective Communication

Write a Skit

Write a skit about two friends on opposite football teams. One friend pushes the other before he or she could catch a pass. Include how the two friends can be good sports towards one another.

Self-Directed Learning

Reading Advertisements

Go to your school library. Look in magazines for tobacco advertisements. How do the advertisements encourage smoking?

Smoking is Cool!

Critical Thinking and Problem Solving

Preventing Asthma Attacks

Your class is voting on a field trip. One classmate suggests the zoo. You know that your friend has asthma and allergies. Write down why the zoo would not be a healthy place for your friend to visit.

Responsible Citizenship

Make a Pamphlet

Make a pamphlet about tobacco. List the types of diseases tobacco smoke can cause and reasons you should not smoke. Put these pamphlets in the school nurse's office and in the cafeteria for students to look through.

Lung Cancer

UNIT E

Community and Environmental Health

CHAPTER 9

Consumer and Community Health, *E2*

CHAPTER 10

Environmental Health, *E22*

CHAPTER 9

Consumer and Community Health

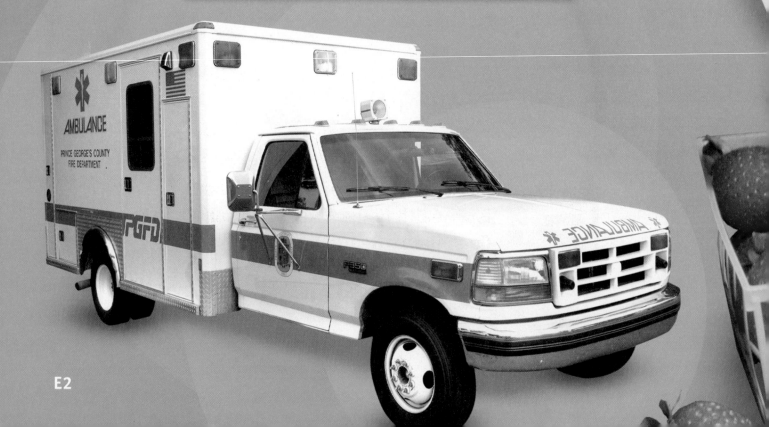

A Healthful Community

Some people in your community work to protect the environment. They work to keep the community clean and healthful.

Most communities have a sanitation (san•uh•TAY•shun) department. Sanitation workers pick up the trash. They might take the trash to a landfill. A *landfill* is a place where waste is buried. The waste is put on material that lines the landfill. The liners keep poisons in trash from leaking into the ground. Sanitation workers might also take the trash to an incinerator (in•SIN•er•ay•ter). An *incinerator* burns waste. Smoke from the incinerator is cleaned before it goes into the air.

Your community also has a health department. Workers there give people shots that help prevent diseases. They make sure restaurants are clean and safe.

 How does the health department help keep the community healthful?

Fighting Pollution

Your community has laws to protect the environment. These laws help keep the environment clean and healthful.

Fighting Air and Water Pollution

Cars and trucks cause air pollution. People can walk places instead of taking a car. This helps keep the air clean.

Most power plants burn oil, gas, or coal to make electricity. Burning these fuels causes air pollution, too. When people use less electricity, they help keep pollution levels down. The power plants will burn less fuel and make less pollution.

Sometimes people need to get rid of paint, chemicals, or other strong cleaners. People may pour them down drains, into toilets, or on the ground. These poisons then can flow into lakes and rivers. Most communities have special collection centers to handle these wastes safely. By using your community's collection center, you fight pollution.

ACTIVITY

On Your Own

FOR SCHOOL OR HOME

Take a Hike

Walking does not cause pollution. It helps keep you fit. Make a list of places you go during the week. Put a check next to the ones you walk to. Show the list to your parent or guardian.

◀ **Pouring paint down a sink drain can cause water pollution.**

Fighting Land and Noise Pollution

Litter causes land and water pollution. You can put your trash in a trash can. This helps keep your community clean.

Do you play loud music? Other people hear the noise you make. This can bother other people. Keep the sound down. This shows respect for others. This helps to keep your environment friendly. This also helps protect your own hearing. Do you listen to loud music through headphones? That can harm your hearing, too. Be sure to keep the volume at a safe level.

 How does using less electricity help protect the environment?

BUILD ACTIVITY
Character
Take Care of the Environment

Respect You show respect for other people by helping to protect the environment. Work with a partner. Plan actions you can take this week to help protect the environment. Can you turn down your radio? Can you recycle your milk carton? Each day, try one action from your plan.

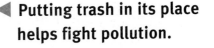

◀ **Putting trash in its place helps fight pollution.**

Saving Natural Resources

MAKE a Difference

Reduce, Reuse, Recycle!

Students in Oregon worked hard to reduce waste. They collected 17,000 milk jugs for recycling. They used scrap paper for note paper. They returned bottles and cans to stores for recycling.

Fighting pollution helps protect the environment. Saving natural resources does, too. You can help save natural resources. One way is to make less trash. You can reduce, reuse, and recycle.

Reduce

To **reduce** is to make less of something. Another word for "reduce" is *precycle*. How could you make less trash? You could put your sandwich in a plastic container instead of plastic wrap. Remember to drink juice from a reusable bottle. Carry your lunch in a lunch box that you can wash each day.

Reuse

To **reuse** is to use items again instead of throwing them away. For example, you could use old jars and milk jugs in new ways. You could keep coins in a jar. You could plant flowers in a milk jug.

▶ Use a lunch box instead of a brown bag to bring your lunch to school.

 **Foldables™** To Learn Life Skills

Learn This Life Skill

Follow these steps to be a health advocate.
The Foldables™ can be used to help.

 1 **Choose a healthful action to communicate.**

Jacob wants to help his brother save electricity.

> Be a Health Advocate
> 1. Choose a healthful action to communicate.
> 2. Collect information about the action.
> 3. Decide how to communicate this information.
> 4. Communicate your message to others.

2 **Collect information about the action.**

Jacob finds out why turning off lights is important to the environment. He records what he finds.

 3 **Decide how to communicate this information.**

Jacob decides to make a poster called "save electricity."

4 **Communicate your message to others.**

Jacob makes his poster. He hangs it in the kitchen for everyone to see.

Practice This Life Skill

You want to explain to people why they shouldn't litter. Work with a partner. Use the four steps to be a health advocate.

Use Vocabulary

decibel, *E27*

environment, *E25*

litter, *E27*

natural resources, *E25*

noise, *E27*

pollution, *E26*

recycle, *E35*

reduce, *E34*

Choose the correct term from the list to complete each sentence.

1. Trash that is thrown on land or in water is __?__.

2. To reuse trash, you must __?__.

3. Substances in the environment that can harm health are __?__.

4. A measure of the loudness of sound is a(n) __?__.

5. Everything around you is the __?__.

6. A loud or constant sound is called __?__.

7. Materials found in nature that are necessary or useful for life are __?__.

8. To __?__ is to make less of something.

Review Concepts

Answer each question in complete sentences.

9. Explain why litter can be unhealthful.

10. Name two types of pollution.

11. Why is saving natural resources important?

12. How can walking or riding a bike help prevent pollution?

13. How do sanitation workers help keep your community clean and healthful?

Reading Comprehension

Answer each question in complete sentences.

Water is cleaned at *water treatment plants* before people use it. At many plants, water flows into a big tank. It sits still there. Some of the dirt in the water sinks. It drops to the bottom of the tank. Cleaner water leaves the tank and flows through sand. The sand traps the rest of the dirt. It also traps some germs. Then workers add a chemical to the water. This kills germs that might still be in the water.

14. What is a water treatment plant?

15. Why is sand used in the plants?

16. How are the germs in the water killed?

Critical Thinking/Problem Solving

Answer each question in complete sentences.

Analyze Concepts

17. You are walking down the sidewalk. A line of firetrucks race down the street. Their sirens and horns are very loud. What should you do?

18. There is pollution in a lake. Some people fish in the lake. Why is this unhealthful?

19. A faucet in your home is dripping. You can't turn it off. What should you do?

20. A car is parked at the curb. Oil slowly drips from its engine. How could this cause water pollution?

21. You have a stack of used worksheets from school. What should you do with them?

Practice Life Skills

22. **Make Responsible Decisions** You are helping your older brother change the oil in his car. Your brother says to dump the old oil into the creek behind your house. Use the *Guidelines for Making Responsible Decisions*™ to make a responsible decision.

23. **Be a Health Advocate** Suppose you want students in your school to make less waste. Make a list of ways you can advocate for this.

Read Graphics

The table below shows how people use water. Use it to answer questions 24–25.

Water Used Each Day in Homes	
Uses For Water	**Number of Gallons Per Person**
bathing	about 14
flushing the toilet	about 20
clothes washer	about 15
dishwasher	about 1

24. Which uses more water, washing clothes or washing dishes?

25. Based on the chart, about how much water per person is used daily?

 LOG ON www.mmhhealth.com
Find out how much you now know about the environment.

Effective Communication

Write a Story

Write a story about a third grader's day. Describe what he or she does during the day to help protect the environment.

Self-Directed Learning

Learn About a Career

Choose a health career that interests you. Go to the library. Read about the career. Write a report and present it to your class.

Critical Thinking and Problem Solving

Quiz a Partner

Write a set of questions about community health. Ask how health helpers work to protect the community. Ask how to prevent pollution. Trade quizzes with a classmate.

Community Health Quiz
1. True
2. False
3. False
4. True
5. False

Responsible Citizenship

Make a Poster

Make a poster to promote recycling. Show how recycling helps the environment.

Glossary

 Visit **www.mmhhealth.com** for an audio glossary in English and in Spanish.

A

accident something that is not supposed to happen (p. C43)

ad a notice that tells people about a product (p. B51)

adolescence (ad•uh•LES•uhns) the stage of the life cycle from age 12 to age 18 (p. B5)

alcohol a drug found in some drinks that slows down the mind and body (p. D11)

allergy (AL•ur•gee) the body's over reaction to a substance (p. D48)

antibody (AN•ti•bod•ee) a substance in the blood that kills germs (p. D41)

apologize say you are sorry (p. A27)

asthma (AZ•muh) a condition in which air passages become narrow (p. D49)

attitude the way you think, act, or feel (p. A20)

B

bacteria (bak•TEER•ee•uh) a one-celled germ (p. D35)

body language the way you move your body to communicate (p. A47)

body system a group of organs that work together to do a certain job (p. B8)

brain an organ that receives and sends messages to all parts of your body (p. B28)

C

caffeine (kaf•EEN) a drug that speeds up body actions (p. D25)

cancer a disease in which cells grow in ways that are not normal (p. D51)

carbon dioxide (KAR•buhn digh•AHK•syd) a gas that is a waste product from your cells (p. B18)

cavity a hole in a tooth (p. C6)

cell the smallest living part of the body (p. B8)

checkup a medical exam to make sure you are healthy (p. C5)

GLOSSARY

chronic disease a disease that lasts for a long time or keeps coming back (p. D47)

clinic a place where you can get medical care without having to stay in a hospital (p. E12)

cocaine (koh•KAYN) an illegal drug that is made from the coca plant (p. D27)

communicate to share feelings, thoughts, or information (p. A47)

community a place where a group of people live (p. E12)

communicable (kuh•MYEW•ni•kuh•buhl) **disease** disease that can be spread to people from other living things or the environment (p. D35)

conflict a disagreement (p. A51)

consumer a person who buys and uses products and services (p. E5)

cool-down five to ten minutes of easy physical activity done after a workout (p. C28)

crack an illegal drug that is a form of cocaine (p. D27)

decibel a measure of the loudness of sounds (p. E27)

dental floss a string-like material used to remove food and dental plaque stuck between teeth and under gums (p. C7)

dental plaque a sticky material that forms on teeth (p. C6)

dependence a strong need for something (p. D17)

diabetes (digh•uh•BEE•tis) a chronic disease in which there is too much sugar in the blood (p. D50)

diet the foods and drinks you digest (p. B39)

Dietary Guidelines suggested goals to help you stay healthy (p. B45)

digestion (digh•JES•chuchn) the process of changing food into a form your body can use (p. B23)

disability something that changes a person's ability to do certain tasks (p. A67)

drug a substance, other than food, that changes how your mind or body works (p. D5)

drug abuse the unsafe use of a medicine or an illegal drug on purpose (p. D9)

drug misuse the unsafe use of a medicine that is done by accident (p. D9)

ear canal leads from your outer ear to your eardrum (p. C12)

eardrum the thin tissue that is stretched like the top of a drum inside your ear (p. C12)

earthquake a shaking or trembling of the ground (p. C56)

ecstasy (EK•stuh•see) an illegal drug that can speed up what happens inside the body (p. D27)

emergency a situation in which help is needed quickly (p. C69)

emotion a feeling inside you (p. A17)

energy the ability to do the work (p. B39)

environment (en•VIGH•run•mint) everything that is around you (p. E25)

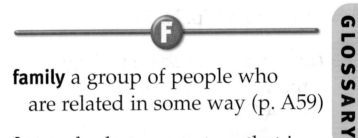

family a group of people who are related in some way (p. A59)

fever a body temperature that is higher than normal (p. D38)

fire escape plan a map of your home that shows different ways out of every room (p. C45)

first aid the quick care given to a person who is injured or is suddenly ill (p. C73)

first aid kit supplies used to care for a person who is injured or ill (p. C77)

flexibility the ability to bend and move easily (p. C22)

flood the overflow of water onto normally dry land (p. C56)

food label a list of ingredients and nutrition facts (p. B52)

friend a person who likes and supports you (p. A65)

G

gang a group of people involved in acts that are dangerous and against the law (p. C65)

germ a tiny particle that can cause disease (p. D35)

good character acting in ways that show healthful traits, such as caring and respect (p. A23)

grooming taking care of your body and appearance (p. C16)

H

harmful stress stress that harms health or causes you to perform poorly (p. A37)

hazard something that can cause harm or injury (p. A43)

health the condition of your body, mind, and relationships (p. A5)

health behavior contract a written plan to help you practice a healthful behavior (p. A8)

health care product something that is used to promote health (p. C16)

health department the local agency that oversees public health (p. E12)

health goal something that you work toward in trying to stay healthy (p. A8)

health helper a person who helps you stay healthy (p. E11)

healthful stress stress that helps you perform well and stay healthy (p. A36)

heart an organ that pumps blood (p. B17)

heart disease a disease of the heart or blood vessels (p. D51)

heart fitness the condition of your heart and blood vessels (p. C22)

heredity the traits you get from your birth parents (p. A11)

hero a person you look up to because of something the person has done or does (p. A24)

hospital a place where ill or injured people are treated (p. E12)

I

I-message a healthful way to talk about feelings when you are upset (p. A18)

immune (i•MYEWN) **system** the body system that protects the body from disease (p. D41)

ingredient (in•GREE•dee•uhnt) an item that goes into making foods or drinks (p. B52)

inhalant (in•HAY•luhnt) a chemical that is breathed into the lungs (p. D26)

injury damage or harm done to a person (p. C43)

Internet a network that connects computers around the world (p. E7)

J

joint the place where two or more bones meet (p. B13)

L

life cycle the stages of life from birth to death (p. B5)

life skill a healthful action you learn and practice for life (p. A7)

litter trash that is thrown on the land or into the water (p. E27)

low body fat having a lean body without too much fat (p. C22)

lungs organs that put oxygen into the blood (p. B18)

M

marijuana (mayr•uh•WAH•nuh) an illegal drug that contains harmful chemicals (p. D26)

media sources of news and information (p. E7)

medicine (MED•uh•sin) a drug used to treat, prevent, or cure an illness or injury (p. D42); (p. D5)

memories things remembered from the past (p. A59)

mouthguard an object worn to protect the mouth and teeth (p. A32)

muscle (MUH•suhl) a type of tissue in the body made of strong fibers (p. B11)

muscle endurance the ability to use your muscles for a long time (p. C22)

muscle strength the ability of your muscles to lift, pull, kick, and throw (p. C22)

MyPyramid a guide that tells the amounts from each food group your body needs every day (p. B40)

natural resources materials found in nature that are necessary or useful for life (p. E25)

nerve cells cells in the sense organs that carry messages to your brain (p. B27)

nicotine (NI•kuh•TEEN) a drug found in tobacco that speeds up the body and forces the heart to beat faster (p. D17)

noise a loud or constant sound (p. E27)

nutrient (NEW•tree•uhnt) a material in a food or drink that is used by the body (p. B39)

organized put together in an orderly way (p. E16)

oxygen a gas needed for you to live (p. B18)

over-the-counter (OTC) medicine a medicine that adults can buy without a doctor's written order (p. D6)

peer someone who is the same age as you (p. A54)

peer pressure the effect that children your age have on you (p. A54)

personal flotation device an object that helps you stay afloat in water; also called a PFD (p. C52)

personality how you look, think, act, and feel that make you different from everyone else (p. A11)

physical fitness having your body in top condition (p. C21)

physical fitness plan a written plan of physical activities (p. C27)

poison a drug or substance that harms or kills (p. C47)

pollution (puh•LOO•shuhn) substances in the environment that can harm health (p. E26)

prescription (prih•SKRIP•shuhn) **medicine** a medicine that your doctor writes an order for (p. D6)

puberty (PYEW•buhr•tee) the time when your body becomes able to reproduce (p. B6)

relationship a connection you have with another person (p. A45)

reliable information information based on scientific study (p. E6)

resistance skills ways to say "no" to unwise decisions (p. A30)

respect treating others as you want to be treated (p. A12); (p. A45)

responsible decision a choice you make that is safe, healthful, and follows family guidelines (p. A29)

reuse to use items again instead of throwing them away (p. E34)

rule a guide to help you do the right thing (p. A12)

R

recycle to change trash so it can be used again (p. E35)

reduce to make less of something (p. E34)

S

safety equipment equipment that protects you from injuries when you play sports or exercise (p. C32)

seat belt the lap-and-shoulder belt worn in a car (p. C49)

secondhand smoke smoke that a person breathes out or the smoke from a burning cigarette, cigar, or pipe (p. D18)

self-concept the feelings you have about yourself (p. A12)

self-control having control over your emotions and actions (p. A18)

skeleton (SKE•luh•tuhn) the framework of your bones (p. B12)

skin an organ that covers your body (p. C15)

snack food eaten between meals (p. B48)

spinal cord a long column of nerve cells that carries messages to and from your brain (p. B29)

spoiled food that is unsafe to eat (p. B59)

stranger someone you do not know well (p. C62)

stress the way your body reacts when there are changes in your life (p. A35)

stressor something that causes stress (p. A35)

sunscreen put on the body to block the sun's harmful rays (p. C15)

symptom a change in your body that is a sign of disease (p. D38)

thunderstorm a storm that has thunder and lightning (p. C56)

tissue cells that work together (p. B8)

tobacco a plant that contains many harmful chemicals, such as nicotine (p. D17)

tornado a powerful storm with winds that whirl in a dark cloud (p. C57)

unsafe touch a touch that is wrong (p. C63)

V

vaccine (vak•SEEN) a substance made with dead or weak germs (p. D41)

values ideas that guide the way a person acts (p. A24); (p. A60)

violence harm done to yourself, others, or property (p. C61)

virus (VIGH•ruhs) a very tiny particle that can reproduce only when it is inside a living cell (p. D35)

vision the sense of sight (p. C11)

vitamin a nutrient that helps your body use other nutrients (p. B39)

W

warm-up three to five minutes of easy physical activity done before a workout (p. C28)

weapon an object that is used to harm someone (p. C66)

GLOSSARY

Glosario

A

accident/accidente Evento inesperado que puede causar daño. (pág. C43)

ad/anuncio Mensaje que avisa sobre un producto o evento. (pág. B51)

adolescence/adolescencia Etapa del crecimiento de los 12 a los 18 años de edad. (pág. B5)

alcohol/alcohol Droga depresiva que se encuentra en algunas bebidas. (pág. D11)

allergy/alergia Reacción negativa del cuerpo ante una sustancia. (pág. D48)

antibody/anticuerpo Sustancia en la sangre que ayuda a combatir gérmenes que entran al cuerpo. (pág. D41)

apologize/disculparse Pedir perdón por una acción que afecta negativamente a otros. (pág. A27)

asthma/asma Enfermedad crónica en la cual las vías respiratorias más pequeñas se estrechan. (pág. D49)

attitude/actitud Manera de pensar, actuar y sentir de una persona. (pág. A20)

B

bacteria/bacteria Germen de una sola célula. (pág. D35)

body language/lenguaje corporal Movimientos o gestos que una persona hace para comunicarse con los demás. (pág. A47)

body system/sistema corporal Grupo de órganos que funcionan en conjunto para realizar un trabajo determinado. (pág. B8)

brain/cerebro Órgano que recibe y envía mensajes a todas las partes del cuerpo. (pág. B28)

C

caffeine/cafeína Estimulante legal que acelera las acciones del cuerpo. (pág. D25)

cancer/cáncer Enfermedad en la cual las células dañinas crecen en forma anormal. (pág. D51)

carbon dioxide/dióxido de carbono
Gas inodoro e incoloro que es un producto de desecho de las células. (pág. B18)

cavity/caries Cavidad de los dientes que comienza en el esmalte. (pág. C6)

cell/célula Parte viva más pequeña del cuerpo de una persona. (pág. B8)

checkup/control médico Examen que realiza un doctor para conocer la salud de una persona. (pág. C5)

chronic disease/enfermedad crónica Enfermedad que dura bastante tiempo o que se repite. (pág. D47)

clinic/clínica Lugar donde una persona puede recibir atención médica sin tener que permanecer allí. (pág. E12)

cocaine/cocaína Droga ilegal que se extrae de las hojas de coca. (pág. D27)

communicable disease/enfermedad contagiosa Enfermedad que puede transmitirse a una persona desde otro ser vivo o el ambiente. (pág. D35)

communicate/comunicar Intercambiar o compartir sentimientos, pensamientos o información con otras personas. (pág. A47)

community/comunidad Lugar donde vive un grupo de personas. (pág. E12)

conflict/conflicto Desacuerdo o pelea. (pág. A51)

consumer/consumidor Persona que compra y usa productos y servicios. (pág. E5)

cool-down/enfriamiento De 5 a 10 minutos de actividad física ligera al terminar el ejercicio. (pág. C28)

crack/crack Droga ilegal derivada de la cocaína. (pág. D27)

decibel/decibel Medida de la intensidad de los sonidos. (pág. E27)

dental floss/hilo dental Hilo que sirve para remover los residuos de alimentos que quedan entre los dientes. (pág. C7)

dental plaque/placa dental Película invisible y pegajosa producida por bacterias que se forma sobre los dientes. (pág. C6)

dependence/dependencia Gran necesidad de algo. (pág. D17)

diabetes/diabetes Enfermedad crónica que se presenta cuando hay mucha azúcar en la sangre. (pág. D50)

diet/dieta Alimentos que una persona ingiere a diario. (pág. B39)

Dietary Guidelines/Pautas Dietéticas Metas sugeridas para alimentarse de manera saludable. (pág. B45)

digestion/digestión Proceso de transformación de los alimentos ingeridos que hace el cuerpo para poder usarlos. (pág. B23)

disability/discapacidad Incapacidad de una persona para ejecutar una acción. (pág. A67)

drug/droga Sustancia no alimenticia que cambia la manera de funcionar del cuerpo o la mente. (pág. D5)

drug abuse/abuso de sustancias Uso de una droga ilegal o uso perjudicial e intencional de un medicamento legal. (pág. D9)

drug misuse/uso indebido de medicamentos Uso peligroso y accidental de un medicamento. (pág. D9)

ear canal/conducto auditivo Canal que conecta el oído externo con el tímpano. (pág. C12)

eardrum/tímpano Membrana situada en el oído que vibra cuando llegan las ondas de sonido. (pág. C12)

earthquake/terremoto Sacudimiento o temblor del suelo. (pág. C56)

ecstasy/éxtasis Droga ilegal que puede acelerar las funciones corporales. (pág. D27)

emergency/emergencia Situación en la que se necesita ayuda inmediatamente. (pág. C69)

emotion/emoción Sentimiento fuerte de una persona. (pág. A17)

energy/energía Capacidad para hacer un trabajo. (pág. B39)

environment/ambiente Todo lo que rodea a una persona. (pág. E25)

family/familia Grupo de personas emparentadas de alguna forma. (pág. A59)

fever/fiebre Temperatura corporal más alta de la normal. (pág. D38)

fire escape plan/plan de evacuación en caso de incendio Conjunto de pasos y opciones para evacuar un lugar. (pág. C45)

first aid/primeros auxilios Atención rápida que se da a un persona herida o enferma. (pág. C73)

first aid kit/kit de primeros auxilios Elementos que se usan para atender a una persona herida o enferma. (pág. C77)

flexibility/flexibilidad Capacidad para doblar y mover el cuerpo con facilidad. (pág. C22)

flood/inundación Desbordamiento de una masa de agua sobre terreno normalmente seco. (pág. C56)

food label/rótulo nutricional Lista de ingredientes e información de nutrición. (pág. B52)

friend/amigo Persona que tiene afecto y apoya a otra. (pág. A65)

gang/ganga Grupo de personas involucradas en actos peligrosos e ilegales. (pág. C65)

germ/germen Ser vivo diminuto que puede causar una enfermedad. (pág. D35)

good character/buen carácter Manera de ser y actuar de una persona que muestra rasgos saludables, como el cuidado y el respeto hacia los de más. (pág. A23)

grooming/aseo Mantenerse limpio y bien presentado. (pág. C16)

H

harmful stress/estrés nocivo Estrés que perjudica la salud o lleva a un desempeño deficiente. (pág. A37)

hazard/riesgo Algo que puede causar daño o lesión. (pág. C43)

health/salud Estado del cuerpo y la mente de una persona, y la manera de relacionarse con los demás. (pág. A5)

health behavior contract/ compromiso de comportamiento saludable Plan escrito que ayuda a una persona a tener un comportamiento saludable. (pág. A8)

health-care product/producto para el cuidado de la salud Artículo que se usa para mantener la buena salud. (pág. C16)

health department/Departamento de Salud Agencia local que supervisa la salud pública. (pág. E12)

health goal/meta de salud Objetivo que una persona busca alcanzar para estar más sana. (pág. A8)

health helper/asistente de la salud Persona que ayuda a las demás a mantenerse saludables. (pág. E11)

healthful stress/estrés saludable Estrés que ayuda a una persona a desempeñarse bien y estar sana. (pág. A36)

heart/corazón Órgano del cuerpo que bombea la sangre. (pág. B17)

heart disease/enfermedad cardiovascular Enfermedad del corazón o los vasos sanguíneos de una persona. (pág. D51)

heart fitness/corazón sano Estado saludable del corazón y los vasos sanguíneos. (pág. C22)

heredity/herencia Rasgos que se heredan de los padres biológicos. (pág. A11)

hero/héroe Persona a quien se admira por algo que ha hecho o hace. (pág. A24)

hospital/hospital Lugar donde personas enfermas o heridas reciben tratamiento. (pág. E12)

I

I-message/mensaje inteligente
Manera saludable de hablar
acerca de los sentimientos
cuando se está enfadado.
(pág. A18)

**immune system/sistema
inmunológico** Sistema que ayuda
a proteger al cuerpo de
enfermedades. (pág. D41)

ingredient/ingrediente Sustancia
que entra en la composición de
un producto. (pág. B52)

inhalant/inhalante Sustancia
química que se aspira. (pág. D26)

injury/lesión Daño o detrimento
corporal causado a una persona.
(pág. C43)

Internet/Internet Red que conecta
computadoras en todo el mundo.
(pág. E7)

J

joint/articulación Punto del cuerpo
donde se unen dos o más huesos.
(pág. B13)

L

life cycle/ciclo de vida Conjunto
de las etapas de la vida desde
el nacimiento hasta la muerte.
(pág. B5)

life skill/destreza para la vida
Acción saludable que se aprende
y se practica para mejorar y
mantener la salud. (pág. A7)

litter/desperdicio Basura que se
arroja al suelo o al agua y que
contamina el ambiente.
(pág. E27)

**low body fat/bajo nivel de grasa
corporal** Estado del cuerpo de
una persona cuando es delgada
y tiene poca grasa corporal.
(pág. C22)

lung/pulmón Cada uno de los
órganos que proporcionan
oxígeno a la sangre. (pág. B18)

M

marijuana/marihuana Droga
ilegal que contiene sustancias
químicas perjudiciales.
(pág. D26)

media/medios de comunicación
Fuentes de noticias e
información. (pág. E7)

medicine/medicamento Droga legal
que se usa para prevenir, tratar o
curar una enfermedad o lesión.
(págs. D42, D5)

memories/recuerdos Eventos del
pasado que vienen a la memoria.
(pág. A59)

mouthguard/protector bucal Objeto
que se usa para proteger la boca
y los dientes. (pág. A32)

muscle/músculo Tipo de tejido
del cuerpo formado por fibras
fuertes. (pág. B11)

**muscle endurance/resistencia
muscular** Capacidad para usar
los músculos durante un tiempo
prolongado. (pág. C22)

muscle strength/fuerza muscular
Capacidad de los músculos
para levantar, tirar, golpear
y lanzar objetos con fuerza.
(pág. C22)

MyPyramid/MiPirámide Guía que
indica las cantidades de cada
grupo alimenticio que necesita
el cuerpo de una persona
diariamente. (pág. B40)

N

natural resource/recurso natural
Material que se encuentra en la
naturaleza y que es necesario o
útil para la vida. (pág. E25)

nerve cell/célula nerviosa Cualquiera
de las células conductoras del
sistema nervioso. (pág. B27)

nicotine/nicotina Droga estimulante que
se encuentra en el tabaco. (pág. D17)

noise/ruido Sonido alto o
constante. (pág. E27)

nutrient/nutriente Sustancia en los
alimentos o bebidas que usa el
cuerpo. (pág. B39)

O

organized/organizado Se dice
de lo que forma un conjunto
ordenado. (pág. E16)

**over-the-counter (OTC) medicine/
medicamento de venta libre**
Medicamento que los adultos
pueden comprar sin receta del
médico. (pág. D6)

oxygen/oxígeno Gas que el cuerpo
necesita para vivir. (pág. B18)

P

peer/compañero Persona de la
misma edad. (pág. A54)

peer pressure/presión de los compañeros Influencia que los compañeros ejercen sobre alguno de ellos. (pág. A54)

personal flotation device/flotador Objeto que ayuda a permanecer a flote en el agua. (pág. C52)

personality/personalidad Manera única de una persona de lucir, pensar, actuar y sentir que la diferencia de los demás. (pág. A11)

physical fitness/buen estado físico Estado óptimo del cuerpo de una persona. (pág. C21)

physical fitness plan/plan para ponerse en forma Plan escrito de actividades físicas. (pág. C27)

poison/veneno Sustancia que daña o mata. (pág. C47)

pollution/contaminación Presencia de sustancias en el ambiente que puede perjudicar la salud. (pág. E26)

prescription medicine/medicamento con receta Medicamento que sólo se puede comprar con una orden del médico. (pág. D6)

puberty/pubertad Etapa de la vida en que el cuerpo de una persona cambia y queda apto para la reproducción. (pág. B6)

R

recycle/reciclar Transformar basura de modo que pueda usarse otra vez. (pág. E35)

reduce/reducir Disminuir algo. (pág. E34)

relationship/relación Vínculo que una persona tiene con otra. (pág. A45)

reliable information/información confiable Información basada en estudios científicos. (pág. E6)

resistence skills/destrezas de resistencia Maneras de decir NO a comportamientos arriesgados. (pág. A30)

respect/respetar Tratar a otros como uno quisiera ser tratado. (págs. A12, A45)

responsible decision/decisión responsable Elección segura y saludable y que cumple con las normas familiares. (pág. A29)

reuse/reutilizar Usar nuevamente algo, en lugar de desecharlo. (pág. E34)

rule/norma Guía que ayuda a hacer lo correcto. (pág. A12)

safety equipment/equipo de seguridad Conjunto de elementos que protegen a una persona de lesiones cuando practica deportes o realiza alguna otra actividad física. (pág. C32)

seat belt/cinturón de seguridad Correa que sujeta a una persona por el hombro y la cintura mientras viaja en un automóvil. (pág. C49)

secondhand smoke/humo de segunda mano Humo que proviene de una persona que fuma o de un cigarrillo, un cigarro o una pipa encendidos. (pág. D18)

self-concept/autoconcepto Opinión que una persona tiene de sí misma. (pág. A12)

self-control/autocontrol Dominio que una persona tiene de sus emociones y sus acciones. (pág. A18)

skeleton/esqueleto Estructura formada por los huesos. (pág. B12)

skin/piel Órgano que cubre el cuerpo. (pág. C15)

snack/refrigerio Alimento que se ingiere entre una comida y otra. (pág. B48)

spinal cord/médula espinal Conjunto de células nerviosas que transporta mensajes desde y hacia el cerebro. (pág. B29)

spoiled/descompuesto Se dice de un alimento que no es apto para comer. (pág. B59)

stranger/desconocido Persona a quien no se conoce bien. (pág. C62)

stress/estrés Forma en que responden el cuerpo y la mente ante los cambios o exigencias de la vida. (pág. A35)

stressor/factor estresante Algo que causa estrés. (pág. A35)

sunscreen/filtro solar Crema o loción que se aplica sobre la piel para bloquear el efecto de los rayos nocivos del Sol. (pág. C15)

symptom/síntoma Cambio en el cuerpo de una persona que es señal de una enfermedad. (pág. D38)

T

thunderstorm/tormenta eléctrica
Tormenta acompañada de
relámpagos y truenos. (pág. C56)

tissue/tejido Grupo de células que
funcionan en conjunto. (pág. B8)

tobacco/tabaco Planta que contiene
sustancias perjudiciales para las
personas, como la nicotina.
(pág. D17)

tornado/tornado Tormenta
poderosa con vientos que giran
en forma de embudo. (pág. C57)

U

unsafe touch/contacto inapropiado
Contacto que no es correcto.
(pág. C63)

V

vaccine/vacuna Sustancia hecha
con gérmenes muertos o
debilitados que da inmunidad
contra determinada enfermedad.
(pág. D41)

values/valores Ideas que guían el
comportamiento de una persona.
(págs. A24, A60)

violence/violencia Daño que una
persona se causa a sí misma, a
los demás o a bienes. (pág. C61)

virus/virus Agente microscópico
que sólo puede reproducirse
cuando está dentro de una célula
viva. (pág. D35)

vision/vista Capacidad de ver.
(pág. C11)

vitamin/vitamina Nutriente que
ayuda al cuerpo a usar otros
nutrientes. (pág. B39)

W

warm-up/calentamiento Actividad
física ligera que se hace por 3 a
5 minutos antes de los ejercicios.
(pág. C28)

weapon/arma Objeto que se usa
para hacer daño a alguien.
(pág. C66)

Index

Note: A page number in *italic* type means there is an illustration on that page.

U

V

T

Credits

Cover and title page photography: Dot-Box for Macmillan/McGraw-Hill

Illustration Credits: Barb Cousins: B08, D11, B11, B12, D17, B17, B19, B23, B28, C06 D49. Jim Spence/Illustrator Represented by Bookmakers: C08, C09, C18, C44, C45, C49, C50, C76. Chris Vallo: A09, A15, A18, A19, A23, A48, A55, B25, C69, D29, E08, E13, E29. Christine M. Schneider: A32, A56, B32, B56, C36, D22, D44, E18, E36. Annie Bissett: B24.

Photography Credits: All photographs are by Macmillan/McGraw-Hill (MMH) except as noted below.

v: bc Joel Benjamin Photography for MMH. vi: bc Victoria Blackie/Getty Images. vii: bl Sonny Senser sonnyphoto.com for MMH. viii: bl Julie Toy/Getty Images. x: bc Kevin Dodge/Masterfile. xi: bc Roy Morsch/CORBIS. xii: bl Richard Hutchings Photography for MMH. i: c Dot-Box for Macmillan/McGraw-Hill. A01: cr, cl, bl, tr, tl, br Richard Hutching Photography for MMH. B01: tr, tl, br Richard Hutchings Photography for MMH. C01: br, cl, bcr, bl, tl, tr Richard Hutchings Photography for MMH. D01: tl, br, bl, cl, tr Richard Hutchings Photography for MMH. E01: tr, br, bc, bl, tl Richard Hutchings Photography for MMH. B01: bl, bl, cl Richard Hutchings Photography for MMH. A02: bl David Young-Wolff/PhotoEdit; tl Stone/Getty Images; tr Siede Preis/Getty Images. D02: tl Jack Holtel Photographik Company for MMH. cr Photodisc Green/Getty Images; bl David Michael Zimmerman/CORBIS; tr Royalty-Free/CORBIS. B02: tc Superstock; bl The Mazer Corporation; tl Image Bank/Getty Images; br Jack Holtel Photographik Company for MMH. C02: tl Lars Klove/Getty Images; bl Richard Hutchings Photography for MMH; t Felicia Martinez/PhotoEdit; br Royalty-Free/Getty Images. E02: cr Photodisc Green/Getty Images; b Tom Carter/PhotoEdit; tl William Whitehurst/CORBIS. A03: bl David Young-Wolff/PhotoEdit; tr Royalty-Free/CORBIS. C03: cr Felicia Martinez/PhotoEdit; c Photodisc Blue/Getty Images. D03: tr Royalty-Free/CORBIS; bl Christina Kennedy/PhotoEdit; br Jack Holtel Photographik Company for MMH. E03: tr YMCA National Safe Place; bl Michelle Garrett/CORBIS. C04: br BSIP Agency/Index Stock Imagery. D04: bc Sonny Senser sonnyphoto.com for MMH. B04: br Chris Windsor/Getty Images. A04: b Ariel Skelley/CORBIS. E04: br Sonny Senser sonnyphoto.com for MMH. A05: bl, br, bc Sonny Senser sonnyphoto.com for MMH. D05: br Sonny Senser sonnyphoto.com for MMH. B05: tr Victoria Blackie/Getty Images; tr SW Production/Index Stock Imagery; cr Royalty-Free/CORBIS; br Stewart Cohen/Getty Images; br IT International ltd./EStock Photo. E05: cr Jack Holtel Photographik Company for MMH. C05: br Photodisc Blue/Getty Images. A06: tl Royalty-Free/SuperStock. E06: bl Richard Hutchings Photography for MMH. D06: cl Jose Luis Pelaz, Inc./CORBIS. B06: br Jose Luis Pelaez,Inc./CORBIS. C07: cr Brian Hagiwara/Getty Images; t Luc Hautecoeur/Getty Images; tr ImageSource Limited/Index Stock Imagery; cr Able Stock/Index Stock Imagery; br Eric Kamp/Index Stock Imagery; b Royalty-Free/CORBIS. E07: br SuperStock. D07: t Jack Holtel Photographik Company for MMH. B07: br Rubberball Productions/Getty Images. B08: tr Rubberball Productions/Getty Images. B09: tr Ross Whitaker/Getty Images. C10: bc Royalty-free/Getty Images. E10: br David Young-Wolff/PhotoEdit. D10: b Sonny Senser sonnyphoto.com for MMH. A10: br Sonny Senser sonnyphoto.com for MMH. B10: br Joel Benjamin Photography for MMH. C11: bl Will and Deni McIntyre/Getty Images. A11: cr, tc, bc Sonny Senser sonnyphoto.com for MMH. B11: cr Diaphor Agency/Index Stock Imagery. A12: br Richard Hutchings/Hutchings Photography. C12: bl Richard Hutchings Photography for MMH. D12: b Mahaux Photography/Getty Images. B12: cl Joel Benjamin Photography for MMH. A13: bc Roy Morsch/CORBIS. C13: c Arthur S. Aubry/Getty Images. E13: cl David Young-Wolff/PhotoEdit. B13: c Bill Bachmann/Index Stock Imagery. A14: bl Rob Lewine/CORBIS. C14: b Sonny Senser sonnyphoto.com for MMH. E14: bc Lisette Le Bon/SuperStock. D14: cl Joel Benjamin Photography for MMH. B14: br Burke/Triolo Productions/Getty Images. C15: bc Michael Keller/CORBIS. E15: br Burazin/Masterfile. D15: cr Nicole Katano/ImageState. A16: bc D.Berry/PhotoLink/Photodisc Green/Getty Images. C16: bl Sonny Senser sonnyphoto.com for MMH; bc Animals, Animals/Earth Scenes. D16: b Bonnie Kamin/PhotoEdit. E16: bl Joel Benjamin Photography for MMH. B16: br Sonny Senser sonnyphoto.com for MMH. C17: bl, br Joel Benjamin Photography for MMH. E17: tr Sonny Senser sonnyphoto.com for MMH. B17: tr Joel Benjamin Photography for MMH. A17: br Joel Benjamin Photography for MMH. C18: bc Myrleen Ferguson Cate/PhotoEdit. D18: bc, br James Steveson/Photo Reseachers Inc. D19: br VOISIN/Photo Researchers; bl The Beauty Archive/EStock Photo; br Index Stock Imagery; bl Paul Barton/CORBIS. A19: bc Joel Benjamin Photography for MMH. B19: bl Dan Bigelow/Getty Images. C19: tc Myrleen Ferguson Cate/PhotoEdit. A20: bl Taxi/Getty Images. C20: br Stephen Simpson/Getty Images. B20: cl Brad Hitz/Stone/Getty Images. D20: br Kevin Dodge/Masterfile. C21: bl Ariel Selley/CORBIS. D21: tr Sonny Senser sonnyphoto.com for MMH. B21: tr Sonny Senser sonnyphoto.com for MMH. B22: b Pictor/ImageState. C22: cl Pam Francis/Getty Images. cl Joel Benjamin Photography for MMH; tl Eric Sanford/Index Stock Imagery; cl D. Berry/Photolink/Getty Images; bl Frank Siteman/Index Stock Imagery. A22: bc Joel Benjamin Photography for MMH. E22: br Photodisc Green/Getty Images; bc Jack Holtel Photographik Company for MMH; cl Gary D. Ercole/Index Stock Imagery; tl Michael Newman/PhotoEdit. A23: bl Joel Benjamin Photography for MMH; B23: br Brian Pieters/Masterfile. E23: tc Chris McElcheran/Masterfile; cl Royalty-Free/CORBIS. A24: bl Tony Anderson/Taxi/Getty Images. C24: b Sonny Senser sonnyphoto.com for MMH. D24: c Richard Hutchings Photography for MMH. E24: b Inga Spence/EStock Photo. C25: br Richard Hutchings/CORBIS. D25: bc Sonny Senser sonnyphoto.com for MMH. E25: cr C Squared Studios/Getty Images. A25: br The Mazer Corporation. A26: br Masterfile. B26: br Photodisc Green/Getty Images. E26: tl Ed Pritchord/Getty Images; b Chris Ladd/Getty Images. A27: tr Ron Fehling/Masterfile. D27: b BananaStock/SuperStock. C27: cr Yellow Dog Productions/Getty Images. E27: b George Hall/CORBIS. A28: b Black Star Images. C28: br Francisco Cruz/SuperStock. D28: bc Joel Benjamin Photography for MMH. B28: cl Index Stock Imagery. E28: bl D. Rose/Masterfile; cl Photodisc Collection/Getty Images. C29: tr Sonny Senser sonnyphoto.com for MMH. E11: Michele D. Bridwell/PhotoEdit.

R30

B29: br Sonny Senser sonnyphoto.com for MMH. A30: br Sonny Senser sonnyphoto.com for MMH. C30: bc Joel Benjamin Photography for MMH. B30: tr Photodisc Green/Getty Images; bl Lawrence Migdale/Photo Researchers. E30: b Kevin Dodge/Masterfile. C31: br Richard Orton/Index Stock Imagery. B31: tc Joel Benjamin Photography for MMH. E31: r Elfi Kluck/Index Stock Imagery. C32: tl Richard Hutchings Photography for MMH. tl Royalty-free/CORBIS; bl, br Joel Benjamin Photography for MMH; bc Sonny Senser sonnyphoto.com for MMH. D32: bl Marlen Raabe/CORBIS; tl Getty Images; br Spike Mafford/Getty Images. E32: bl Hugh Burden/SuperStock. C33: bl Esbin/Anderson/The Image Works; br Joel Benjamin Photography for MMH; bc Myrleen Ferguson Cate/PhotoEdit. D33: tl Siede Preis/Getty Images; br Royalty-Free/CORBIS. E33: b Craig Hammell/CORBIS; tl Strauss/Curtis/CORBIS. A34: b Joel Benjamin Photography for MMH. C34: b Tom and Dee Ann McCarthy/CORBIS; tl Chris Cole/Getty Images. D34: bc Joel Benjamin Photography for MMH. E34: br BananaStock/SuperStock. A35: inset John Burke/SuperStock. D35: br Dr. Dennis Kunkel/Visuals Unlimited; br Dr. George Chapman/Visuals Unlimited; br Veronika Burmeister/Visuals Unlimited; br Dr. Gary Gaugler/Visuals Unlimited; br Barry Runk/Grant Heilman Photography. E35: c Gary D. Ercole/Index Stock Imagery. A36: bl Sonny Senser sonnyphoto.com for MMH; cr, br Joel Benjamin Photography for MMH. B36: bl Foodpix/Getty Images; tr Felicia Martinez/PhotoEdit; tl Jacqui Hurst/CORBIS; c The Image Bank/Getty Images; cr Royalty-Free/Getty Images; br Royalty-Free/CORBIS. A37: bl Sonny Senser sonnyphoto.com for MMH. D37: cr Jerome Tisne/Getty Images. B37: tr Michael Newman/PhotoEdit; tc Steve Lupton/CORBIS; br Amy Etra/PhotoEdit; bl Royalty-Free/CORBIS. A38: br Ian Shaw/Stone/Getty Images. B38: bc Sonny Senser sonnyphoto.com for MMH. D38: cl Rob Lewine/CORBIS. B39: cr SuperStock; br Foodpix/Getty Images; cr Alison Barnes Martin/Masterfile. B40: cr Joel Benjamin Photography for MMH. E40: br Joel Benjamin Photography for MMH; tl Charles Orrico/SuperStock; tr Masterfile (Royalty-Free Div.). D40: b Richard Hutchings Photography for MMH. E40: br Joel Benjamin Photography for MMH. C40: bc Richard Hutchings Photography for MMH; tr Myrleen Ferguson Cate/PhotoEdit; cr Felicia Martinez/PhotoEdit; tl Henry T. Kaiser/Index Stock Imagery; cl Royalty-Free/Getty Images. B41: tl, b, c, c, cl Joel Benjamin Photography for MMH; b, tl Photodisc/Getty Images; c Eisenhut & Mayer/FoodPix/Getty Images. D41: cr Dr. David Phillips/Visuals Unlimited. C41: bl Tony Freeman/PhotoEdit; cr CORBIS; br Photodisc Green/Getty Images; tl Eric Fowke/PhotoEdit. C42: br Sonny Senser sonnyphoto.com for MMH. A42: bl Royalty-Free/Getty Images; cl Jack Holtel Photographik Company for MMH; tr Royalty-Free/CORBIS. B42: cl, tl, bl Joel Benjamin Photography for MMH. B43: tc, c Joel Benjamin Photography for MMH; cr © Francisco Cruz/SuperStock. A43: bl David Young-Wolff/PhotoEdit; tr Felicia Martinez/PhotoEdit. C43: br Richard Hutchings/PhotoEdit. D43: tr Sonny Senser sonnyphoto.com for MMH. A44: br Joel Benjamin Photography for MMH. B44: b Richard Hutching Photography for MMH. C44: cr PhotoEdit; br David Muir/Masterfile; br Joel Benjamin Photography for MMH. B45: bc Sonny Senser sonnyphoto.com for MMH. A46: cl Sonny Senser sonnyphoto.com for MMH. B46: tl, cl, bl SuperStock. C46: bc Royalty-Free/SuperStock. D46: bc Ariel Skelly/CORBIS. B47: tr Thomas Del Brase/Stone/Getty Images; cr Park Street/PhotoEdit. D47: r Amit Bushan. B48: cl Robertstock Retrofile. C48: b Flip Chalfant/Getty Images. D48: bl Michael Keller/Index Stock Imagery; bl Burke/Triolo Productions/Getty Images; bl Alberto Cassio/ImageState; bl Klaus Hackenberg/Getty Images. B49: cr Richard Hutchings Photography for MMH. D49: br Roy Morsch/CORBIS. A49: cr David Schmidt/Masterfile. A50: b Sonny Senser sonnyphoto.com for MMH. B50: b Richard Hutchings Photography for MMH. D50: bl Royalty-Free/CORBIS. A51: cr, br, cr Sonny Senser sonnyphoto.com for MMH. B51: br Ron Chapple/Taxi/Getty Images; br Sonny Senser sonnyphoto.com for MMH; br Grant Heilman Photography, Inc. C51: b Royalty-Free/SuperStock. D51: br Kevin Radford/Masterfile. A52: b Elyse Lewin/Getty Images. B52: bl Robertstock Retrofile. C52: cl Royalty-Free/Getty Images. D52: cl Ron Chapple/Getty Images; br © Jeff Greenberg/Visuals Unlimited. D53: cr PhotoDisc/Getty Images. B54: b Richard Hutchings Photography for MMH. C54: b Tom and Dee Ann McCarthy/CORBIS. C55: bc Julie Toy/Getty Images. C56: cl Royalty-Free/Getty Images. D56: c Ryan McVay/Getty Images; bc G. Staebler/Masterfile. A58: b Joel Benjamin Photography for MMH. B58: bc Sonny Senser sonnyphoto.com for MMH. B59: tc Image Source Limited/Index Stock Imagery; bc Sonny Senser sonnyphoto.com for MMH; c Index Stock Imagery. A59: cr Diana Koenigsberg/Stone/Getty Images; br Hurewitz Creative/CORBIS. A60: br Royalty-Free/CORBIS. C60: b Sonny Senser sonnyphoto.com for MMH. B60: bl Brand X Pictures/Roberstock Retrofile. C61: br, bc Sonny Senser sonnyphoto.com for MMH. B61: cr Jack Holtel Photographik Company for MMH. A62: cl Kevin Dodge/Masterfile. C62: bl Richard Hutchings Photography for MMH. A63: c Christopher Bissell/Stone/Getty Images. A64: bc Jim Corwin/Index Stock Imagery. C64: b Charles Gupton/CORBIS. B64: br FoodPix/Getty Images; bc Brand X Pictures/Getty Images; cr Photographer's Choice/Getty Images; cl Sonny Senser sonnyphoto.com for MMH. A65: tr Joe Gemignani/CORBIS. C65: br Rolf Bruderer/CORBIS. A66: bl Sonny Senser sonnyphoto.com for MMH. A67: bc Lawrence Migdale/Stone/Getty Images. C68: b Greg Smith/CORBIS SABA. A68: cl Friend/Denny/Stockphoto. A69: c Richard Hutchings Photography for MMH. C70: cr Jack Holtel Photographik Company for MMH. C72: br Richard Hutchings/Hutchings Photography. A72: cl Royalty-Free/Getty Images; cr Kevin Dodge/Masterfile; c CORBIS; cr CORBIS; bl Jack Hotel Photographik Company for MMH. C74: bl Richard Hutchings Photography for MMH; b Garo/Photo Researchers; cl © Joe McDonald/Visuals Unlimited. C75: bl Mauritius, GMBH/Phototake; tl © Gary Meszaros/Visuals Unlimited; b H. Stanly Johnson/SuperStock; cl Royalty-Free/Getty Images. C77: cr Jack Holtel Photographik Company for MMH. C80: cr Photodisc Blue/Getty Images; bc, c Jack Holtel Photographik Company for MMH.